WRITER'S RESEARCH HANDBOOK

The Research Bible for Freelance Writers

by Keith M. Cottam and Robert W. Pelton

BARNES & NOBLE BOOKS

A DIVISION OF HARPER & ROW, PUBLISHERS

New York, Hagerstown, San Francisco, London

A hardcover edition of this book is published in the United States by A. S.
Barnes and Co., Inc. It is here reprinted by arrangement.

WRITER'S RESEARCH HANDBOOK: A GUIDE TO SOURCES. Copyright © 1977 by
A. S. Barnes and Co., Inc. All rights reserved. Printed in the United States of
America. No part of this book may be used or reproduced in any manner with-
out written permission except in the case of brief quotations embodied in
critical articles and reviews. For information address A. S. Barnes and Co.,
Inc., Cranbury, New Jersey 08512. Published simultaneously in Canada by
Fitzhenry & Whiteside Limited, Toronto.

First BARNES & NOBLE BOOKS edition published 1978

ISBN: 0–06–463468–X

78 79 80 81 82 10 9 8 7 6 5 4 3

To my wife, Laurel, and my children, Mark, Lisa, Andrea and Brian, for their inspiration, encouragement, support, criticism, and even long-suffering when this book and other writing projects have so unfairly taken "their" time. And without my co-author, Robert Pelton, and my secretary, Jane Gross, the book would never have grown beyond a "Library Resources" guide at the University of Tennessee, Knoxville.

Contents

Preface

Would you like to write a historical novel but don't know where to begin? Want to do a factual nonfiction book? Interested in writing accurate articles for national magazine publication? Doing some short stories based on real-life incidents? Need to work up a good term paper? A master's thesis? Or even a doctoral dissertation?

Groping around for a topic on which to write? Facing a wall in your research? Don't know where to turn for further information? Is that last statistic still eluding your determined search? Or is there something else you want to know about but don't know whom to ask?

Writer's Research Handbook is intended to help solve all of the above problems! And it will answer all your questions. It is geared to aid in locating information from a great variety of fields. Sources providing similar types of information are grouped together for the researcher-writer's convenience. There is even a comprehensive index.

Writer's Research Handbook is truly the ''research Bible'' for all freelance writers. And it is an invaluable tool to have on hand for magazine staff writers, newspaper journalists, and students as well.

Note To The Researcher

This book may seem a little irreverent to alert librarians or skilled researchers who are familiar with all the latest reference books. You will note that dates of publication are omitted for many of the sources. The annotations are short and subjective. Finally, no attempt has been made to be exhaustive.

Don't be discouraged by the lack of publication dates. Many research tools are revised and reissued regularly, and dates of publication quickly become meaningless unless you have the latest edition in hand. So how do you know when you have the latest edition? *Ask an experienced reference librarian!* Your time as a busy researcher and writer is too valuable to waste on personally locating the latest edition of a reference book. For example, if you know you want a particular type of index or directory, ask your librarian for the latest edition. You need information; librarians are trained to place you quickly into the most up-to-date guides.

Designed as a practical companion to help you gather information fast, the book does not dwell on the technical arrangements of reference books or on how to use card catalogs. These things are best learned from a librarian or when you have a book in hand with a motive for using it.

The notations are written to save you time in determining which reference sources appear most useful for your research. Your examination and inquiry will inevitably suggest and lead to the right sources—including sources not listed in this book.

WRITER'S
RESEARCH HANDBOOK

1. Background Information on Your Subject

Encyclopedias tend to get lost in the shuffle of information needs as people grow older and a little more sophisticated. This is unfortunate. Encyclopedias are handy, reliable sources of information. They provide uncomplicated overviews or explanations of thousands of subjects, personalities, or places. They often include references to other important sources of information, thus saving you valuable research time. And they are unusually valuable for quick answers to questions such as who, what, when, where, and why.

If you cannot locate the information you need in one of the familiar General Information Encyclopedias listed, consult a Subject Encyclopedia for more specific or in-depth coverage. Or check one of the dictionaries listed in Chapter 4. Many of them include much more information than simply definitions of words. In addition, there are many other encyclopedias including works in languages from Arabic to Ukranian. Your librarian will tell you if any of these are in the library.

Do you want to buy an encyclopedia for personal use? Librarians usually will not give you advice on the matter. If they do not, ask for the latest edition of *General Encyclopedias in Print* by S. Padraig Walsh. This comparative analysis is published by the R.R. Bowker Company and provides practical guidelines for buying an encyclopedia.

GENERAL INFORMATION ENCYCLOPEDIAS

1. *Collier's Encyclopedia*. New York: Crowell-Collier Educational Corporation. NOTE: You will find this attractive adult encyclopedia less formidable to use than the more intellectual *Americana* (item 3) or the scholarly new *Britannica* (item 4). It is notable for popularly written and timely, factual articles. A separate index volume includes a separate bibliography listing over eleven-thousand widely available books written in English.

2. *The New Columbia Encyclopedia*. New York: Columbia University Press. NOTE: How do you condense the knowledge of the world into one volume? Here is the best 10½ lb. example available. You may not find every bit of information you need; you will find this a valuable single-volume time-saver for thousands of excellent, factual articles. Most are biographical and geographical subjects. There are also maps, tables, illustrations, and over forty-thousand bibliographic references. This encyclopedia is not revised as often as others, so use it as a basic retrospective source. Older editions such as the 1963 *Columbia Encyclopedia* include articles excluded from this new 1975 edition.

3. *Encyclopedia Americana*. New York: Americana Corporation. NOTE: Use this basic source for finding authoritative information quickly about most subjects, particularly for unique facts on American history, geography, and biography. A comprehensive index volume is the key to thousands of subjects that

do not have separate articles. An annual yearbook supplements the basic set.

4. *Encyclopedia Britannica,* 15th ed. Chicago: Encyclopedia Britannica, Inc. NOTE: Here is an all new concept in encyclopedias, primarily because of its three separate parts. The ten volume "Micropaedia" is a concise fact finder and index key to the long, scholarly articles in the nineteen volume "Macropaedia." "Propaedia" presents an ambitious "outline of the whole human knowledge."

5. *Encyclopedia International.* New York: Grolier, Inc. NOTE: The tabular presentation of information, color plates, and the large number of articles with specific entries make this useful as a fast, general reference source.

6. *Lincoln Library of Essential Information.* Columbus, Ohio: Frontier Press Company. NOTE: New editions are frequently published, which update the thousands of brief, factual articles arranged under twelve general subject fields. The detailed indexes in each of its two volumes will lead you to information in the articles as well as in the charts, tables, bibliographies, maps, and color illustrations.

7. *World Book Encyclopedia.* Chicago: Field Enterprise Educational Corporation. NOTE: *World Book* is the most widely accepted encyclopedia for young people, but because of its content, organization, and style, it is often a preferred choice for researchers who need quick facts or a basic overview. An annual yearbook supplements the basic set.

SUBJECT ENCYCLOPEDIAS

8. *Dictionary of American History.* New York: Charles

Scribner's Sons. NOTE: Turn to this standard seven-volume set for a basic survey of American history — political, economic, social, industrial, and cultural. Volume six is a supplement and covers the period from 1940 to 1960. The revised index, published in 1963, is your key to exploring the six main volumes.

9. *The Encyclopedia of Education*. New York: The Macmillan Company & The Free Press. NOTE: This is the only basic encyclopedia in the field of education. Its documented articles synthesize the history, theory, research, philosophy, and structure of education. Volume 10 is a detailed index.

10. *Encyclopedia of Philosophy*. New York: The Macmillan Company & The Free Press. NOTE: As the major English language encyclopedia of philosophy, it will be found in most research libraries. It is written and indexed primarily for researchers rather than philosophers; and it includes both Oriental and Western concepts.

11. *Encyclopedia of World Art*. New York: McGraw-Hill Book Company, Inc. NOTE: This comprehensive fifteen-volume historical synthesis covers all periods and includes art forms, history, artists, and allied subjects. Over half of each volume is devoted to black and white or color reproductions. The index lists the art as well as textual topics.

12. *Grove's Dictionary of Music and Musicians*. New York: St. Martin's Press, Inc. NOTE: *Grove's* is the standard encyclopedia in the field of music and generally will answer most music-related questions. There is no index, but the alphabetical arrangement and numerous cross-references are usually adequate. A wide-ranging and frequently revised single-volume music reference work is *The International Cyclopedia of Music and Musicians*,

published by Dodd, Mead & Company.

13. *International Encyclopedia of the Social Sciences*. New York: The Macmillan Company & The Free Press. **NOTE:** Do not confuse this with the classic *Encyclopedia of the Social Sciences* published in 1930. The *International* is a totally new standard work that focuses on the concepts, theories, and methods of such subjects as anthropology, economics, geography, history, law, political science, psychiatry, psychology, sociology, and statistics. Volume 17 is a comprehensive index.

14. *McGraw-Hill Encyclopedia of Science and Technology*. New York: McGraw-Hill Book Company. **NOTE:** No other science encyclopedia can compare with this excellent source. Its broad survey articles and shorter definitional entries are useful for either the novice or the expert. A *Yearbook* keeps it up-to-date.

15. Menke, Frank G. *The Encyclopedia of Sports*. New York: A.S. Barnes and Company. **NOTE:** Here is a treasure of sports information that will capture your curiosity. It includes history, descriptions, basic rules, and names and records of champions for nearly eighty sports, ranging from angling to yachting. Another sports encyclopedia is *The Oxford Companion to World Sports & Games,* published by Oxford University Press.

2. Magazine or Newspaper Articles That Have Been Published on Your Subject

The researcher would be lost hopelessly without the indexing and abstracting services that monitor the millions of magazine and newspaper articles published each year. Even if your library does not have the magazines indexed, you can identify the articles and ask for them through interlibrary loan (item 237), or go directly to other libraries nearby. Your librarian will assist you with an interlibrary loan. You can locate other libraries through telephone directories or special directories such as the *American Library Directory* (item 184), *Directory of Special Libraries and Information Centers* (item 189), or *Subject Collections* (item 200).

Indexes list articles according to a system, such as by author, title, or subject. They are of two types: General, such as the *Readers' Guide to Periodical Literature* (item 18); and Subject, such as the *Index to Legal Periodicals* (item 28). There is also a special *Index to U.S. Government Periodicals* (item 173).

Abstracting services also list articles according to some system. In addition, they summarize the essential features and facts of the articles listed.

You will notice that most of the indexes included in this guide are published by the H.W. Wilson Company. It is one of the major reference-book companies and concentrates on indexes to magazines. The company distributes several free descriptive catalogs that are highly useful for the researcher. You should ask for copies: The H.W. Wilson Company, 950 University Ave., Bronx, New York 10452.

Familiarity with Wilson indexes is essential, but awareness of other indexes and abstracts is also important. A representative selection of the more useful available is included in this section. Many others are published that may be of value in your search for information. A list is included in *Ulrich's International Periodicals Directory* (item 224). Consult your library's card catalog to find out whether the library has a certain index or abstract, or save time by asking a librarian. Librarians know which indexes and abstracts they have and where they are shelved in the library.

GENERAL INDEXES

16. *Access; The Supplementary Guide to Periodicals*. Syracuse, New York: Gaylord Bros., Inc., 1975 to date, three times yearly with last issue cumulated. NOTE: Ever wonder where *Playboy* is indexed? Or *TV Guide*? Or maybe *Glamour*? In this new index you will find them for the first time along with over 125 other magazines not included in major existing indexing services. *Access* gives you a key to magazines on entertainment, travel, science fiction, religion, politics, and other subjects, including magazines for children and teens.

17. *Humanities Index*. New York: The H.W. Wilson Company, June 1974 to date, quarterly, annual cumulations. NOTE: This is one of two new in-

dexes that replace *Social Sciences and Humanities Index* (item 20). The other is *Social Sciences Index* (Item 19). Use it to locate reviews of books, plays, musical productions, films, dance, and opera, as well as articles from about 260 magazines. In addition, it can be used as a survey guide to contemporary developments, trends, opinions, and controversies in the humanities. Author and subject entries are arranged in a single alphabet.

18. *Readers' Guide to Periodical Literature*. New York: The H.W. Wilson Company, 1905 to date, semimonthly from September to June, monthly in July and August, quarterly, and annual cumulations. NOTE: Use this with caution. Although it is the best known and most widely used author and subject index to popular magazine articles published in the United States, it does *not* index all general and nontechnical magazines. There is a list in the front of each volume of the nearly 160 magazines it does index. Refer to *Access* (item 16) for another general index to about 130 additional popular magazines. You must use the general indexes with the specialized subject indexes for more comprehensive magazine article research.

19. *Social Sciences Index*. New York: The H.W. Wilson Company, June 1974 to date, quarterly with annual cumulations. NOTE: This new index is one of two that replace the *Social Sciences and Humanities Index* (item 20). The other is *Humanities Index* (item 17). The single alphabet arrangement includes author and subject entries and many cross-references to help you locate articles and book reviews in over 260 magazines.

20. *Social Sciences and Humanities Index*. New York: The H.W. Wilson Company, 1965-1974. NOTE: This

author and subject index replaced the *International Index* (1907-1965). In 1974 it changed again to become two new indexes (items 17 and 19).

SUBJECT INDEXES

21. *Applied Science & Technology Index.* New York: The H.W. Wilson Company, 1958 to date, monthly except July, annual cumulations. NOTE: All the information from more than 220 scientific and technical magazines is indexed by subject. You will be able to locate articles of interest to scientists, technicians, students, and laymen.

22. *Art Index.* New York: The H.W. Wilson Company, 1929 to date, quarterly with annual cumulations. NOTE: *Art Index* will help you locate information on all aspects of the field, including movements, trends, and styles. It provides a complete author and subject index to more than 150 U.S. and foreign magazines.

23. *Biological & Agricultural Index.* New York: The H.W. Wilson Company, September 1964 to date, monthly with quarterly and annual cumulations. NOTE: Keep up with developments in the life sciences through this subject index to nearly 190 magazines. It is useful for locating practical as well as scientific information.

24. *Business Periodicals Index.* New York: The H.W. Wilson Company, 1958 to date, monthly, except August, with quarterly and annual cumulations, NOTE: References on research findings, current developments, trends, products, ideas, methods, and business news from more than 150 magazines are included in this subject index.

25. *Consumers Index to Product Evaluations and Informa-*

tion Sources. Ann Arbor, Michigan: Pierian Press, 1973 to date, quarterly with annual cumulations. NOTE: With this index you not only have a key to the contents of the standard consumer magazines, such as *Changing Times* and *Consumer Reports*, but also to the articles and information of consumer interest in many other magazines, books, and pamphlets. Summaries are included for many of the articles indexed.

26. *Current Index to Journals in Education*. New York: Macmillan Information, 1969 to date, monthly with annual cumulations. NOTE: *CIJE* includes subject, author, and specific journal contents indexing to selected information in about seven-hundred education or related publications. It duplicates much of what you will find in the *Education Index* (Item 27) and is generally available only in larger research libraries.

27. *Education Index*. New York: The H.W. Wilson Company, 1929 to date, monthly, except July and August, with quarterly and annual cumulations. NOTE: This is the most widely used author and subject guide to the entire contents of more than 220 publications in the field, including yearbooks and proceedings.

28. *Index to Legal Periodicals*. New York: The H.W. Wilson Company, August 1952 to date. monthly, except September, with quarterly, annual, and three-year cumulations. NOTE: More that 320 legal periodicals are indexed. The index is divided into three parts: subject and author, table of cases, and book reviews.

29. *Library Literature*. New York: The H.W. Wilson Company, 1921 to date, bimonthly, with annual and two-year cumulations. NOTE: Keep up with the information explosion through this author and subject index to more that two-hundred library and informa-

tion science magazines and related publications.

30. *Music Index*. Detroit: Information Service, 1949 to date, monthly, with annual cumulations. NOTE: More than two-hundred U.S. and European magazines are indexed by author and subject. With this you can also locate music reviews—including performances and recordings—listed under composer, title, and medium.

31. *Public Affairs Information Service Bulletin*. New York: Public Affairs Information Service, 1915 to date. weekly, cumulates five time per year and annually. NOTE: More commonly known as *PAIS*, this index is an indispensable guide to the social sciences. In addition to listing periodical aritcles, it includes books, pamphlets, numerous state and national government documents, factual and statistical reports, and other documentary material. A wide selection of periodicals is indexed. This sets *PAIS* apart from Wilson-type indexes, which cover a limited number of periodicals. Most research libraries will have *PAIS*. Larger libraries will also have the *Cumulative Subject Index to the P.A.I.S. Annual Bulletin, 1915–1975*, published by Carrollton Press, Inc.

ABSTRACTING SERVICES

Usually called abstracts, abstracting services are more difficult to use than the familiar Wilson-type indexes. Most are based on a classified arrangement, which requires you to use additional author, subject, or geographical indexes included with each issue in order to locate a specific reference. They are often confusing to use and you will save time with help from a librarian.

32. *America: History and Life*. Santa Barbara, California: American Bibliographical Center—Clio Press, 1964 to date. NOTE: This progressively expanded and improved source is now a three-part comprehensive current guide to writings in American and Canadian history. Part A, "Article Abstracts and Citations." is issued quarterly and includes subject and author indexes, plus an annual cumulative subject and author index. Part B, "Index to Book Reviews," is issued semiannually. Part C, "American History Index," is an annual comprehensive index to the articles and books cited in Parts A and B, plus a listing of dissertations. Complements *Historical Abstracts* (item 35).

33. *Chemical Abstracts*. Columbus, Ohio: American Chemical Society, 1907 to date, weekly with collective semiannual indexes. NOTE: This is the most comprehensive abstracting service example in the scientific area and includes references to articles, patents, formulas, and new books in the field.

34. *Child Development Abstracts and Bibliography*. Chicago: The University of Chicago Press for the Society for Research in Child Development, 1927 to date, three times per year. NOTE: This is an excellent source for book reviews as well as references to articles on the biological, psychological, and sociological development of children.

35. *Historical Abstracts*. Santa Barbara, California: American Bibliographical Center—Clio Press, 1955 to date. NOTE: *Historical Abstracts* cites articles from all countries and languages except the United States and Canada, which are covered by *America: History and Life* (item 32). With volume 19, 1973, coverage was extended from the period 1775-1945 to include history from 1450 to the present. It is now published in two parts: Part A, "Modern History

Abstracts, 1450-1914,'' and Part B, "Twentieth Century Abstracts, 1914 to the Present.'' Both are issued quarterly with indexes; the fourth issue of each is a cumulative index.

36. *Psychological Abstracts*. Washington, D.C.: American Psychological Association. Inc.. 1927 to date, monthly, with semiannual cumulative indexes. NOTE: This "provides nonevaluative summaries of the world's scientific literature in psychology and related disciplines" from over eight-hundred publications.

37. *Sociological Abstracts*. New York: Sociological Abstracts, Inc., 1953 to date, five issues per year, cumulative indexes. NOTE: Here is the major key to sociological literature, including sources on subjects such as industrial organization, mass communication, ecology, demography, radical sociology, and feminist studies.

NEWSPAPER INDEXES

There are very few published indexes to local newspapers. Some public libraries maintain clipping files. Large newspaper publishers usually support libraries that keep various clipping and index files. Other special libraries and information centers often analyze and catalog specific newspaper information. Ask your librarian for possible leads to these sources, or consult the directories mentioned at the beginning of this chapter.

The Bell and Howell Company (Micro Photo Division, Old Mansfield Rd., Wooster, Ohio 44691), publishes a *Newspaper Index* to several geographically important newspapers. You may find this index in very large research libraries or in libraries where the regional newspapers are significant.

If you are looking for leads to significant local or regional events, the indexes listed here may help. For example, *The New York Times Index* (item 39) is valuable for locating the exact date of an event, checking proper names, or getting the facts of a story as published in *The New York Times*. From there you can turn to *The New York Times* itself or other newspapers and magazines that may have covered the event.

38. *Index to The Christian Science Monitor*. Ann Arbor, Michigan: University Microfilms, 1960 to date, monthly. NOTE: The *Monitor* is well known for its objective, in-depth coverage of national and international affairs.

39. *The New York Times Index*. New York: The New York Times, 1851 to date, semimonthly, with annual cumulations. NOTE: Here is the best quick source of information and perspective on events from the past. Each citation includes a factual abstract of the news story, which frequently eliminates the need to look further for your information. Additional news summary sources are listed in Chapter 11.

40. *The Wall Street Journal Index*. Princeton, New Jersey: Dow Jones Books, Inc., 1958 to date, monthly, with annual cumulation. NOTE: There are two parts to this that you will want to check. One lists articles under the names of companies; the second includes all other references. The newspaper itself is strong in general news coverage as well as in business and economic areas.

3. Books That Have Been Published On Your Subject

Start with your library's card catalog when you want to find a book. But do not be misled into thinking a card catalog is the only source necessary—or even the best. It is usually only an index to *books* located in a specific library. Most books in a library will be listed in the card catalog at least once in alphabetical order under author or title. Many books will also be listed under specific subjects. Ask your librarian for assistance if you are not sure which subject to look under, or if you do not understand the information on a card for a book in which you are interested.

But what about all the books the library does not have? Even the largest research libraries do not have every book published. So, you must rely on a host of special catalogs and bibliographic guides, some of which are listed in this chapter. In addition, magazines, scholarly and professional journals, newspapers, and special book reviewing media regularly cite new publications to help you keep abreast of current materials. Once you know of a new book that your library does not have, you can request that the library buy a copy. If you want an older book your librarian will assist you with an interlibrary loan (item 237).

GENERAL GUIDES TO REFERENCE BOOKS

Librarians know how and where to locate the information you need. If you ask a question for which an answer source does not readily come to mind, they may turn to one of the following examples of reference book guides. These guides are often kept behind the librarian's desk, but there is nothing mysterious about them. Ask for these and others that may be available.

41. *American Reference Books Annual*. Littleton, Colorado: Libraries Unlimited, Inc., 1970 to date, annual. NOTE: Commonly called *ARBA*, this is a comprehensive annual source of reviews for reference books published or distributed in the United States. Reviews describe the content and purpose of each book. They often compare them with similar books and cite additional reviews from other major reviewing sources.

42. Sheehy, Eugene P. *Guide to Reference Books*. Chicago: American Library Association. NOTE: Biennial since 1968, this publication supplements *Guide to Reference Books* (item 43).

43. Winchell, Constance M. *Guide to Reference Books*, 8th ed. Chicago: American Library Association, 1967. NOTE: You will find this standard and unequalled guide to reference resources at the reference desk of nearly every library. When you do not know where to look or have exhausted other sources, "Winchell" is the place to look for direction. It is supplemented by *Guide to Reference Books* (item 42). A revised and enlarged ninth edition of *Guide to Reference Books* will be published by the American Library Association under the byline of Eugene P. Sheehy.

44. Wynar, Bohdan S., ed. *Reference Books in Paperback: An Annotated Guide*. Littleton, Colorado: Libraries Unlimited, 1972. NOTE: A writer can develop an excellent, low-cost personal reference collection with the aid of this selective guide. It describes and evaluates 675 reference books in paperback.

GUIDES TO BOOKS IN SPECIFIC FIELDS

Subject bibliographies, or guides to writings in particular fields, are essential for anyone forging through the often confusing array of books, articles, and other information on a specific topic. As roadmaps to literature-searching, a library or researcher cannot function without them. Representative guides to broad fields are included here. Thousands more are available for specific areas.

If a subject bibliography is available in book form in your library it will usually be listed in the card catalog. Look under the subheading "Bibliography" for the subject. If a quick check of the card catalog does not turn up what you want, ask your librarian for assistance. Other subject bibliographies are included as parts of books and articles. Check *Bibliographic Index* (item 53) for many of these. Your librarian will request an interlibrary loan (item 237) for subject bibliographies it does not have.

If there is not one to match your specific need, you many have to research and compile your own. Your librarian will help outline a search strategy through many sources. These include the library's card catalog, Library of Congress *National Union Catalog,* periodical indexes and abstracts, or the guides to current book publication. Keep in mind that a unique bibliography is a valuable resource. It may result in a potential publication as a by-product of your primary project.

45. Blum, Eleanor. *Basic Books in the Mass Media.* Urbana: University of Illinois Press, 1972. NOTE: The subtitle of this book describes it as "an annotated, selected booklist covering general communications, book publishing, broacasting, film, magazines, newspapers, advertising, indexes, and scholarly and professional periodicals."

46. Burke, Arvid J., and Burke, Mary A. *Documentation in Education.* New York: Teachers College Press, 1967. NOTE: The Burkes revised the fourth edition of an earlier work, *How to Locate Educational Data,* to produce this useful book. It not only emphasizes the literature of education but also includes chapters on bibliographic research methods.

47. Freidel, Frank, ed. *Harvard Guide to American History,* revised edition. Cambridge, Massachusetts: The Belknap Press of Harvard University Press, 1974. NOTE: This basic reference work succeeds a series of predecessors dating back to 1896. Now in two volumes this *Guide* is an expanded finding aid to published sources categorized by topic or period.

48. Lasworth, Earl. *Reference Sources in Science and Technology.* Metuchen, New Jersey: Scarecrow Press, 1972. NOTE: Identify reference books by field with this guide. It is well indexed by author and subject.

49. Malinowsky, Harold R. *Science and Engineering Reference Sources.* New York (now Littleton, Colorado): Libraries Unlimited, 1967. NOTE: This standard reference and library guide is used by students and librarians. Over four-hundred basic reference books in math, physics, chemistry, astronomy, geology, biology, and engineering are described.

50. Modern Language Association. *MLA International Bibliography of Books and Articles in the Modern*

Languages and Literatures. New York: Modern Language Association of America, 1921 to date, annual. NOTE: A researcher cannot conduct serious library research without this vital tool and major source.

51. *The Reader's Adviser.* New York: R.R. Bowker. NOTE: This book lover's bible is the best-known literary source guide published. It is indispensable for literary facts and lore as well as bibliography. The first volume of the greatly expanded twelfth edition was published in 1974 and is a guide to "the best in American and British fiction, poetry, essays, literary biography, bibliography and reference." Two additional volumes covering drama and foreign literature in translation, and all other areas of the social sciences, sciences, and humanities will eventually be published. Earlier editions are indispensable until then.

52. White, Carl M. *Sources of Information in the Social Sciences,* second ed. Chicago: American Library Association, 1973. NOTE: First published in 1964, this quality guide to the literature will be found in any research library. Both editions are useful since different scholars worked on each edition. The newer edition has added a chapter on geography. This is in addition to those on general social sciences, history, economics and business administration, sociology, anthropology, psychology, education, and political science.

AN INDEX TO BIBLIOGRAPHIES

53. *Bibliographic Index.* New York: The H.W. Wilson Company, 1937 to date, semiannual, with yearly

cumulations and irregular permanent cumulated volumes. NOTE: This "cumulative bibliography of bibliographies" is an essential research key that is often
overlooked. If you cannot locate a bibliography
through the card catalog or the guides to reference
books, you have a good chance of identifying one
here. It includes bibliographies published as books as
well as those that are parts of books, pamphlets and
periodical articles, both in English and foreign languages. Large research libraries will also have the
*Cumulative Subject Guide to U.S. Government Bib-
liographies 1924-1973* (item 172). It is published in
seven basic volumes with an annual updating service.

CURRENT BOOK PUBLICATIONS

When you need to know what books are in print, who the
authors are, or what books certain publishers are issuing, the
R.R. Bowker Company will give you the answers. The
Bowker Company is the geographer of the book trade.
Bowker publications are the most convenient sources for
getting all the facts you need on the entire book-publishing
scene.

In addition to the basic catalogs listed below, Bowker
publications include *Literary Market Place* (item 219),
Photography Market Place (item 222), *Fine Arts Market
Place* (item 214), and many other reference books, bibliog-
raphies, and directories. You should keep current copies of
Bowker's catalogs in your personal resource file. Write:
R.R. Bowker Company, 1180 Avenue of the Americas, New
York, New York 10036.

54. *Books In Print*. Annual. NOTE: Commonly called *BIP*,

this lists current books alphabetically by author and by title, with full bibliographic data on each book.

55. *Subject Guide to Books In Print*. Annual. NOTE: Titles from *Books In Print* (item 54) are rearranged and listed under Library of Congress subject headings.

56. *Books In Print Supplement*. Annual. NOTE: This midyear catalog updates the current volumes of *Books In Print* (item 54) and the *Subject Guide to Books In Print* (item 55).

57. *Paperbound Books In Print*. Three times per year. NOTE: The first volume each year is a basic catalog. The second volume supplements it. The third volume cumulates all information added since the basic volume was published.

58. *Children's Books In Print*. Annual. NOTE: Locate authors, titles, publishers, and other bibliographic information with this catalog. It also includes information on grade level, edition, number of volumes, and illustrator for nearly all books for kindergarten through grade twelve levels.

59. *Subject Guide to Children's Books In Print*. Annual. NOTE: This arranges the titles from *Children's Books In Print* (item 58) under subject headings.

60. *Business Books In Print*. Annual. NOTE: Business books are arranged by subject and indexed by author and title.

61. *El-Hi Textbooks In Print*. Annual. NOTE: Textbooks for elementary, secondary, and adult education levels are indexed by subject, title, author, and series.

62. *Bowker's Medical Books In Print*. Annual. NOTE: All kinds of books are included for medicine, nursing, psychiatry, dentistry, veterinary medicine, and para-professional areas. There are three separate indexes: subject, author, and title.

63. *Scientific, Technical, and Engineering Societies Pub-*

lications In Print 1974-1975. NOTE: Basic bibliographic data for publications is arranged under 151 scientific, technical, and engineering societies. This catalog will become obsolete unless issued in further editions.

64. *Weekly Record*. NOTE: Once a part of *Publishers Weekly*, the book industry journal, the *Weekly Record* is now issued as an independent publication. It is *not* a record of books in print. It provides Library of Congress card cataloging data for current American book publications, some of which comes from Cataloging in Publication (CIP) data. CIP records are sometimes produced for books in publication that never reach the market.

65. *American Book Publishing Record*. Monthly. NOTE: Commonly called the *ABPR*, this monthly magazine cumulates by Dewey Decimal subject arrangement all the books listed during the current month in the *Weekly Record* (item 64). The twelve monthly issues are cumulated into an *ABPR Annual Cumulative*, which includes separate sections for juvenile books and fiction.

66. *Forthcoming Books*. Bimonthly. NOTE: Each issue cumulates titles of new books published since the last issue of *Books In Print* (item 54), and forecasts books to be published during the next five months. It includes an author list and a title list.

67. *Subject Guide to Forthcoming Books*. Bimonthly. NOTE: A subject arranged companion to *Forthcoming Books* (item 66).

68. *Publishers' Trade List Annual*. NOTE: Do you need to know what books are published by certain publishers? Here is a convenient compilation of publisher's catalogs to give you the answers. It is commonly call *PTLA*.

69. *Cumulative Book Index*. New York: The H.W. Wilson Company, 1928 to date, monthly, except August, with annual cumulations. NOTE: Commonly called *CBI*, it represents a basic cumulated retrospective record of books published in the English language. (Bowker publications, on the other hand, list only American publications.) Authors, titles, and subjects are in a single alphabetical arrangement, with the author entry giving complete bibliographic information.

BOOK REVIEWS

Save time with book reviews. Learn what the critics are saying about a new book. Refresh your memory about a book without rereading it. Compare and evaluate books even though you do not have them readily at hand.

Busy readers know the value of book reviews published in such sources as *The New York Times Book Review, The New York Review of Books,* and many other popular magazines and scholarly journals. Librarians regularly appraise new books with the help of special library publications such as *Booklist, Choice, Library Journal, ARBA* (item 41), and *Reference Services Review*. Not all review sources are the same, of course. Some are long, critical essays, while others very in length and may be largely descriptive. If you are not familiar with book review sources, ask your librarian for help in identifying the best for your needs.

Reviews are sometimes difficult to locate after they have been published. Most reviews are indexed in one or more of the following sources: *The New York Times Index* (item 39) also cites reviews, and you will find reviews listed in periodical indexes. For example, *Readers' Guide* (item 18) lists some under subject and author. Subject indexes, such as

Biological and Agricultural Index (item 23), *Index to Legal Periodicals* (item 28), and *Child Development Abstracts and Bibliography* (item 34), feature special book review sections. In other fields, book reviews are best approached by way of the author of the work in such sources as *Art Index* (item 22) and *Library Literature* (item 29). Or, some libraries will have *Current Book Review Citations*—a new time-saving index published by the H.W. Wilson Company. It brings together review citations included in ten Wilson indexes, as well as citations from other selected publications. Variations of how reviews are listed occur in almost all indexes. Ask your librarian for assistance.

70. *Book Review Digest*. New York: The H.W. Wilson Company, 1905 to date, monthly, except February and July, with annual cumulations. NOTE: This is the basic source for locating reviews. Excerpts from reviews of the more popular fiction and nonfiction books are given with citations to the complete reviews.

71. *Book Review Index*. Detroit: Gale Research Company, 1965 to date, bimonthly, with annual cumulations. NOTE: Reviews are indexed from all the major literary and educational journals, as well as from many magazines that review books on arts and crafts, business and economics, religion, philosophy, and current affairs. The Gale Research Company also publishes the *Children's Book Review Index,* which is based on the reviews mentioned in the *Book Review Index*.

72. *An Index to Book Reviews in the Humanities*. Williamson, Michigan: Phillip Thomson, 1960 to date, annual. NOTE: All reviews (except children's books) from humanities periodicals are indexed.

73. *Technical Book Review Index*. New York: Special Li-

braries Association, 1965 to date, monthly. NOTE: Books reviewed in scientific, technical, and trade journals are indexed, including excerpts from the reviews.

INDEXES TO ANTHOLOGIES AND COLLECTIONS

Do you need to find part of a book such as a poem? A short story? Or maybe a play? Here are four special indexes that analyze the contents of books and other literature collections.

74. *Essay and General Literature Index*. New York: The H.W. Wilson Company, 1900 to date, semiannual with annual cumulations. NOTE: Many libraries use this author and subject index as a buying guide to books of essays and other collections. A list of selections for inclusion in the index are even sent each month to index subscribers. Literary criticism is emphasized, although nearly all areas of knowledge are included, particularly the social sciences and humanities.

75. *Granger's Index to Poetry,* 6th ed. New York: Columbia University Press, 1973. NOTE: Use this as your first approach to locating poetry from hundreds of anthologies in four different ways. Three alphabets cover title and first line, author, and subject.

76. *Ottemiller's Index to Plays in Collections*. 5th ed. Metuchen, New Jersey: Scarecrow Press, 1971. NOTE: This is "an author and title index to plays appearing in collections published between 1900 and mid-1970." Many of the sources indexed are out-of-print and will be available only through interlibrary loan. Ask your librarian for assistance.

77. *Short Story Index*. New York: The H.W. Wilson Company, 1953 to date. NOTE: Prior to 1975 this index was issued six times in five-year volumes and included only stories in collections. With its publication as an annual beginning in 1975, the index provides a key to stories in collections *and* periodicals. The publisher still plans to issue permanent five-year cumulations. Stories are indexed by author, title and subject in one alphabet.

4. Definitions

A good dictionary is the most treasured information source a writer can possess. In practice, unless you have a command of the entire English language, several types of word-reference books will become priceless for your work. First, a thumb-indexed "college" dictionary is popular for personal reference collections. It will save you immeasurable time in pinning down spelling, definitions, syllabication, pronunciation, variants, usage, derivation, and synonyms and antonyms. In addition, the better dictionaries include abbreviations, slang terms, foreign words and phrases, biographical and geographical names, and quotations. They also contain information of an encyclopedic nature such as charts, tables, and illustrations.

A "college" dictionary will not include all the enormous vocabulary in the English language. Sometimes you must turn to an unabridged dictionary. Every library has at least one of these located prominently on a stand. You will find *Webster's Third New International Dictionary of the English Language* in most libraries, or perhaps its predecessor, *Webster's New International Dictionary of the English Language*. Other unabridged dictionaries include *Funk & Wagnalls New Standard Dictionary, The American Heritage*

Dictionary of the English Language, and the *Random House Dictionary of the English Language.* Each is generally useful, yet each is unique. As your librarian for clarification of the differences.

In addition, there are hundreds of special subject dictionaries that will help you understand the nuances of the English language. Many simply define words, but others are similar to encyclopedias, which include lengthy essays, bibliographies, and illustrations. Thus, the right dictionary will serve many purposes. Ask your librarian for other dictionaries not included here.

SUBJECT DICTIONARIES

78. *Black's Law Dictionary.* St. Paul, Minnesota: West Publishing Company. NOTE: Although revised only four times since 1891, this remains the standard law dictionary in most reference libraries.

79. Brandon, S.G.F., ed. *A Dictionary of Comparative Religion.* New York: Charles Scribner's Sons, 1970. NOTE: Use this for encyclopedic information as well as definitions. Many entries also include bibliography and cross-reference to related topics.

80. Cowan, Henry J. *Dictionary of Architectural Science.* New York: John Wiley & Sons, 1973. NOTE: Entries range from one line to more than one page. Terms are taken from architecture, fine art, building trades crafts, engineering, materials science, physics, and chemistry. The book also includes seven appendices and illustrations.

81. English, Horace B., and English, Ava Champney. *A Comprehensive Dictionary of Psychological and Psychoanalytical Terms.* New York: David McKay Company, 1958. NOTE: This "guide to usage" is the

most popular work of its kind. Concise definitions.

82. *Funk & Wagnalls Standard Dictionary of Folklore, Mythology, and Legend*. New York: Funk & Wagnalls Publishing Company, 1972. NOTE: The subject of this dictionary is so vast that only a cross section is included. Many of the articles include references to related literature, but you may need to ask your librarian for additional reference books on the subject.

83. Good, Carter V., ed. *Dictionary of Education*. New York: McGraw-Hill Book Company. NOTE: Periodic updating of this work since 1937 makes it the most valuable record of educational terms from all fields. Definitions are clear and concise.

84. Gould, Julius, and Kolb, William L., eds. *A Dictionary of the Social Sciences*. New York: Free Press, 1964. NOTE: This is the best single-volume dictionary available on the language of social science. Each definition is signed by the author.

85. Hastings, James, ed. *Dictionary of the Bible*. rev. ed. New York: Charles Scribner's Sons, 1963. NOTE: Based on the Revised Standard Version with cross references to King James and Revised Versions. This work includes all proper names mentioned in the Old Testament as well as biblical doctrines and theological concepts.

86. Kent, Ruth Kimball. *The Language of Jounalism: A Glossary of Print-Communications Terms*. Ohio: The Kent State University Press, 1970. NOTE: Designed as a teaching aid, this handy reference book will even help practicing journalists sort the jargon of their trade. Illustrations supplement many definitions. Sections on "sources consulted" and "bibliography" of additional reference sources are bonus features.

87. Kohler, Eric L. *A Dictionary for Accountants*. Englewood Cliffs, New Jersey: Prentice-Hall. NOTE: Periodic editions of this since 1952 improves its value. The language of accounting is explained with illustrations as well as definitions, so that even nonaccountants can grasp its meaning.

88. *McGraw-Hill Dictionary of Art*. New York: McGraw-Hill Book Company, 1969, in five volumes. NOTE: The *Encyclopedia of World Art* (item 11) is the best art source available, but this dictionary cannot be matched as a quick reference source, particularly for biography. It also includes 2,300 illustrations, four-hundred of which are in color.

89. *McGraw-Hill Dictionary of Modern Economics; a Handbook of Terms and Organizations.* 2nd ed. New York: McGraw-Hill Book Company, 1973. NOTE: In addition to defining about 1,400 economic terms, descriptions are given for some 225 public, private, and nonprofit associations, agencies, and research organizations concerned with economics and marketing. Other references to sources of information are included with many of the definitions.

90. *McGraw-Hill Dictionary of Scientific and Technical Terms*. New York: McGraw-Hill Book Company, 1974. NOTE: If scientific language has you baffled, this is the best dictionary to help you bridge your communication gap. It includes nearly 100,000 concise definitions with additional diagrams, charts, symbols, photographs, drawings, and other special features.

91. Plano, Jack C., and Greenberg, Milton. *The American Political Dictionary*. rev. and expanded. New York: Holt, Rhinehart and Winston, 1967. NOTE: Terms are arranged alphabetically within subject chapters, which is an unusual arrangement for a dictionary.

Use the index to locate the definition and analysis of the term you need.

92. Shipley, Joseph T., ed. *Dictionary of World Literary Terms*. Boston: The Writer, 1970. NOTE: This is a revision of an earlier work called *Dictionary of World Literature*. Definitions cover terms, forms, techniques, types, and genres. There are also critical surveys of American literature as well as others.

93. *Stedman's Medical Dictionary*. New York: Charles Scribner's Sons. NOTE: Librarians, students, medical personnel, and laymen turn to this frequently revised and classic dictionary for help with life-science vocabulary. It is illustrated and includes an alphabetical index to subentries, appendices, tables, eponyms, and synonyms.

HISTORICAL DICTIONARIES

The meanings and interpretations of words often change. With an historical or etymological dictionary in hand you can trace the changes from the time a word was first used. If you cannot locate or trace the meaning of a particular word in the following, ask your librarian for additional sources.

94. Craigie, Sir William A., and Hulbert, James R., eds. *A Dictionary of American English on Historical Principles*. Chicago: The University of Chicago Press, 1938–1944, 4 volumes. NOTE: Craigie modeled this work after the famous *The Oxford English Dictionary* (item 96), the dictionary on which he worked earlier as an editor. Craigie's dictionary supplements *The Oxford English Dictionary* for American English.

95. Mathews, Mitford M., ed. *A Dictionary of Amer-*

icanisms on Historical Principles. Chicago: The University of Chicago Press, 1951. NOTE: This dictionary traces the history of words peculiar to America. Use it to supplement *The Oxford English Dictionary* (item 96) and the *Dictionary of American English on Historical Principles* (item 94).

96. *The Oxford English Dictionary*. Oxford, England: Clarendon Press, 1933, 13 volumes. NOTE: Usually called the *OED*, this scholarly classic is seldom used for simple definitions or spelling. It is out-of-date for new words, but those included are given encyclopedic treatment. One reviewer of the work explained that

> what one finds in it are not cut-and-dried definitions of words resting in peace, but the lives of words—their births, maturations, fadings into feeble old age and occasional deaths.

The *OED* is best used to study the lives of British English words. Use *A Dictionary of American English on Historical Principles* (item 94) or *A Dictionary of Americanisms on Historical Principles* (item 95) for American English.

SLANG AND DIALECT DICTIONARIES

Slang dictionaries are the "humble" companions to other dictionaries of more traditional or conventional language. You may not find them in some public and school libraries. In other libraries you must ask for them as they are placed discretely out of reach.

97. Partridge, Eric. *A Dictionary of Slang and Unconventional English*. New York: Macmillan Publishing

Company. NOTE: Periodic revisions and supplemented editions of this work keep it up-to-date.
The subtitle of the reprinted seventh edition (1974)
explains that the dictionary covers "colloquialisms
and catch-phrases, solecisms and catachreses, nick-
names, vulgarisms, and such Americanisms as have
been naturalized."

98. Wentworth, Harold, and Flexner, Stuart Berg.
Dictionary of American Slang. New York: Thomas
Y. Crowell. NOTE: Supplemented editions of this
keep you abreast of contemporary language. It is
notable for the inclusion of obscenities, vulgar, and
taboo words, with examples of usage, quotations,
and etymologies.

SYNONYMS AND ANTONYMS

Along with your favorite conventional dictionary you
probably turn most frequently to a dictionary of synonyms.
These word finders help you expand your vocabulary or find
another word for one you have used too many times.

99. Hayakawa, S. I. *Funk & Wagnalls Modern Guide to
Synonyms and Related Words*. New York: Funk &
Wagnalls, 1968. NOTE: Do not turn to this for a quick
reference. Key words and main synonyms are noted
in the margin with accompanying essays explaining
the various uses. Many words you want will be cited
only in the essays that are the heart of the work. Use
the index and "copious cross-references" to find the
right words.

100. Rodale, J.I., ed. *The Synonym Finder*. Emmaus, Pennsylvania: Rodale Books, 1961. NOTE: Use this with
caution. It is convenient and popular with many

writers because of the extensive number of possible synonyms compiled under each alphabetically arranged key word. But the editors have taken the license to include many words that have different meanings in different contexts.

101. *Roget's International Thesaurus*. New York: Thomas Y. Crowell. NOTE: Dating back to 1852, *Roget's* groups words differently than the usual dictionary in which you start with words and look for meanings. Here you find words grouped according to related ideas. You must use the index. Also, unless you already have a fair command of English, *Roget's* can be difficult and confusing to use. Most writers will turn first to *Webster's New Dictionary of Synonyms* (item 102). An interesting variation on the thesaurus theme is found in *Bernstein's Reverse Dictionary* published by Quadrangle.

102. *Webster's New Dictionary of Synonyms*. Springfield, Massachusetts: G.&C. Merriam Company. NOTE: *Webster's* overcomes some of the problems encountered in *Funk & Wagnalls Modern Guide to Synonyms and Related Words* (item 99), *The Synonym Finder* (item 100), and *Roget's International Thesaurus* (item 101). It is not a mere word-finding list. It is not a collection of essays on word usage. Words are arranged in alphabetical order with appropriate synonyms and antonyms. Shades of meanings are carefully explained and illustrated.

ABBREVIATIONS AND ACRONYMS

You will find basic abbreviations and acronyms in general dictionaries. But save time by referring directly to one of the following. There are also other sources. Ask your librarian for assistance.

103. *Acronyms and Initialisms Dictionary*. Detroit, Michigan: Gale Research Company. NOTE: Frequently revised, this "guide to alphabetic designations, contractions, acronyms, initialisms, and similar condensed appellations" covers subjects, associations, and activities.

104. *New Acronyms and Initialisms*. Detroit, Michigan: Gale Research Company. NOTE: Yearly issues cumulate with the last edition and supplement the latest edition of the *Acronyms and Initialisms Dictionary* (item 103).

105. *Reverse Acronyms and Initialisms Dictionary*. Detroit, Michigan: Gale Research Company. NOTE: Acronyms and initialisms do not always mean what they appear to mean. Here they are arranged alphabetically by what they actually mean or represent, rather than by the abbreviation itself. It is a valuable companion volume to *Acronyms and Initialisms Dictionary* (item 103).

106. Wall, C. Edward. *Periodical Title Abbreviations*. Detroit, Michigan: Gale Research Company, 1969. NOTE: This handy guide will help you solve the mystery of those abbreviated magazine titles so often included in footnotes or other references.

USAGE AND STYLE MANUALS

How do you deal with the English language in a concise, accurate, and vigorous manner? What are the rules of usage and the principles of composition? There are numerous manuals and guides to answer such questions. Each is designed to meet particular needs. Students in college English courses may use the *Harbrace College Handbook* as a text. Journalists may keep a well-used copy of *The Associated Press Stylebook* or some similar publication close at hand.

The University of Chicago's *Manual of Style* is the authority
for many writers, while others rely on Kate Turabian's
Manual for Writers. And *Words Into Type,* published by
Prentice-Hall, Inc., is an old reliable authority for writers,
editors, proofreaders, and printers.

There are numerous other such modern guides to be used
alongside the two standards listed below. Ask your librarian
for those in the library.

107. Fowler, H.W. *A Dictionary of Modern English Usage.*
Second edition revised by Sir Ernest Gowers. New
York: Oxford University Press, 1965. NOTE: The
rules and regulations governing proper usage of the
English language are prescribed in Fowler's classic
guide. Most dictionaries simply describe or record
language as it is used.

108. Strunk, William J., and White, E.B. *The Elements of
Style.* Second Edition. New York: The Macmillan
Company, 1972. NOTE: Here is the most popular
book of sensible advice for any writer. In addition to
the rules of usage, principles of composition, and
reminders for style, it is a classic in its own right —
fascinating just to read. Two other books that deal
with faulty rhetoric and grammar are Edwin
Newman's *Strictly Speaking* and Jacques Barzun's
Simple & Direct.

RHYMING DICTIONARY

109. Stillman, Frances. *The Poet's Manual and Rhyming
Dictionary.* New York: Thomas Y. Crowell, 1965.
NOTE: If you are into writing poetry you probably
avoid rhyming dictionaries. But if you are not a poet,
and simply need words that rhyme with other words
for some reason, here is a good reference book.

5. Fact Sources: Almanacs, Handbooks, Yearbooks, and Manuals

Current almanacs—those intriguing collections of data and statistics on people, places, events, and subjects—are surpassed only by good dictionaries as treasured information sources for writers. These fact books are designed to give you quick answers to current as well as historical questions. Most are full of miscellaneous facts. Some are highly useful for general encyclopedic features; yet others are published to cover special subjects. As with your favorite dictionary you eventually will settle on a favorite almanac. Popular titles include *Information Please Almanac* (item 117) or *The World Almanac and Book of Facts* (item 125). Check a reference book guide such as *Guide to Reference Books* (item 43) to learn of other titles.

Your librarian will use a variety of fact books when concerned with such needs as a chronology of events, a display of facts about countries or governments, a table of statistics, or a summary of information on other specific subjects. Do not assume information is not available if *you* cannot locate it. Too many fact books are easily overlooked. If you cannot quickly find the answer you want in one source, check another or ask for assistance. For example, you may overlook the usually obscure but valuable compendiums of information found in encyclopedia yearbooks. Yearbooks for general encyclopedias include the *Americana Annual* (item 3) and *The World Book Yearbook* (item 7). The *McGraw-Hill Yearbook of Science and Technology* supplements the *McGraw-Hill Encyclopedia of Science and Technology* (item 14).

See also the statistics sources listed in Chapter 8. Such references as the *Statistical Abstract of the United States* (item 154), the United Nations *Demographic Yearbook,* or the *Editor & Publisher Market Guide* are rich in concise, quick reference information.

Directory sources such as the *Official Congressional Directory* (item 146) and even your telephone directory will often provide the right answers. So use your imagination and combine the use of almanacs, handbooks, yearbooks, and manuals with encyclopedias, dictionaries, directories, and other sources. In this way you will meet a majority of your information needs.

110. Barone, Michael. *Almanac of American Politics*. Boston: Gambit, 1972 to date, new edition for each Congress. NOTE: You can find the same information in other sources. But the authors have compiled what you need on the subject to produce the most readable single volume of its kind. Try, for example, to locate information quickly in the *Official Congressional Directory* (item 146) or other government publications, and you will return to this new reference for its convenience. It not only gives the facts on legislators and constituencies, but also gives a rundown on the political pulse, economy, and other areas of political interest for each state.

111. *The Book of the States.* Lexington, Kentucky: The Council of State Governments, 1935 to date, biennial. NOTE: Use this for the states as the *Municipal Year Book* (item 122) is used for cities. It is most useful for narrative and tabular data on governmental and administrative organization, working methods, and financial and functional activities. Supplements issued between the basic volumes present comprehensive lists of state officials and legislators.

112. *The Bowker Annual of Library and Book Trade Information.* New York: R.R. Bowker, 1955 to date, annual. NOTE: Statistics, articles on trends, and reports and news from various areas of librarianship and publishing make up this annual. It also includes directory information for both fields, as well as events calendars and lists of award-winning books and authors.

113. *Congress and the Nation.* Washington, D.C.: Congressional Quarterly, Inc. NOTE: Volumes in this series are published periodically and provide summaries of legislation and political activity for specific periods of time. Greater detail on specific legislative actions and political trends are found in the *Congressional Quarterly Almanac* (item 114).

114. *Congressional Quarterly Almanac.* Washington, D.C.: Congressional Quarterly, Inc., 1945 to date, annual. NOTE: This is a convenient compendium of legislative activity for each session of the U.S. Congress. *Congress and the Nation* (item 113) and *CQ Weekly Reports* (item 180) are companion references. Some volumes of the *Almanac* (e.g., 1973, 1974) include a useful "glossary of Congressional terms" and a description of "how a bill becomes law." The *Congressional Record* with its *Index* (item 170) is the official daily record of the proceedings of Congress.

Check *CQ Weekly Report* (item 180) for a current summary of Congressional activity. For a record of who's who in the U.S. Congress look in the *Official Congressional Directory* (item 146) and the *Congressional Staff Directory* (item 145).

115. *Countries of the World and Their Leaders*. Detroit, Michigan: Gale Research Company. NOTE: The subtitle of this book describes it as

> the U.S. Department of State's report on status of the world's nations, combined with its series of background notes portraying contemporary political and economic conditions, governmental policies and personnel, political parties, religion, history, education, press, radio and TV, and other characteristics of each nation. Includes Central Intelligence Agency's list of chiefs of state and cabinet members of foreign governments.

116. *The Europa Year Book*. London: Europa Publications Limited, 1926 to date, annual. NOTE: World political organization and economics are covered in two authoritative volumes: international organizations and Europe in volume one; Africa, the Americas, Asia and Australia in volume two. If you cannot locate the information you need in this reference. check *The Statesman's Year Book* (item 123).

117. *Information Please Almanac, Atlas and Yearbook*. New York: Information Please Almanac, annual. NOTE: The "atlas and yearbook" part of the title are somewhat misleading. Not all the information you would expect to find in an atlas or a yearbook are found in this or any other almanac. But this is a good source for facts on thousands of subjects. What you do not find in this almanac you may find in *The World Almanac and Book of Facts* (item 125) or other sources.

118. *International Motion Picture Almanac*. New York: Quigley Publications Company, 1929 to date, annual. NOTE: Start with this handbook when you want to know anything about the movie industry. It includes a who's who, plus many lists and directories. The index is at the front of the book.

119. *International Television Almanac*. New York: Quigley Publications Company, 1956 to date, annual. NOTE: The needs of the television industry are served with this convenient reference. It will provide the information you need or lead you to other sources through its lists and directories. The index is at the front of the book.

120. Kane, Joseph N. *Famous First Facts*. 3rd ed. New York: H.W. Wilson Company, 1964. NOTE: You many find yourself spending more time than you save with this. The facts cover happenings, discoveries, and inventions. They are indexed by years, by days of the month, by personal names, and by geographical location. Kane is also the author of *Facts About the Presidents,* another indispensable source for browsers as well as researchers.

121. McWhirter, Norris, and McWhirter, Ross, Eds. *The Guiness Book of World Records*. New York: Sterling Publishing Company. NOTE: Originally produced as a catalog of facts with which to settle various arguments, *Guiness* has become the standard by which new records are attempted—and perhaps more arguments started. But couple this book with Kane's *Famous First Facts* (item 120), a good dictionary and your favorite general almanac, and you will not only settle arguments, but will also add valuable bits of information to your writing.

122. *The Municipal Year Book*. Washington, D.C.: International City Management Association, 1934 to date,

annual. NOTE: Use this for municipal data as *The Book of the States* (item 111) is used for the states. Data for specific cities is presented only as it relates to the issues being analyzed in each annual volume. The major concerns analyzed from year to year are not the same. The current volume is most useful as a quick reference for its directories of municipal officials. A full section of additional sources will guide further research.

123. *The Stateman's Year-Book*. New York: St. Martin's Press, 1864 to date, annual. NOTE: This "statistical and historical annual of the states of the world" is the authoritative information source on every country and territory. It covers such topics as history, area and population, government, religion, justice, social services, finance, defense, agriculture, industry, labor, commerce, banking, communications, and transportation. Compare this source with *The Europa Year Book* (item 116) when doing research in any of these areas.

124. *United States Government Manual*. Washington, D.C.: Government Printing Office, 1935 to date, annual. NOTE: The title of this official handbook of the federal government was changed with the 1973–74 issue from the long familiar *United States Government Organization Manual* to the present title. It is particularly useful for addresses as well as descriptions (including organization charts) of the purposes and programs of most government agencies. Use the *Almanac of American Politics* (item 110) or the *Official Congressional Directory* (item 146) for better coverage of the legislative branch of government or congressional activities.

125. *The World Almanac and Book of Facts*. New York: Newspaper Enterprise Association, 1868 to date,

annual. **NOTE:** *The World Almanac* is often cited as the foremost single-volume reference book. In practice, the best source is the one that meets your specific information needs, and it may be the *Information Please Almanac, Atlas and Yearbook* (item 117) or an entirely different reference book. Useful information in *The World Almanac* is located easily through the index at the front of the book.

6. Information About People: Biography

Information about people is included in nearly everything you read or write. Sometimes the information is crafted into a complete book about a person's life. Many times, biographical anecdotes are used to give life to articles. Other writing requires the inclusion of facts about a person, which help to explain a specific subject, an historical event, or the circumstances of a particular period of time.

Biographical information is one of the most useful and popular forms of knowledge to be found in familiar as well as unfamiliar places. Your daily newspaper, for example, is filled with biographical references as diverse as gossip columns, obituaries, and feature stories. But how to you tap this rich source?

One newspaper, *The New York Times,* publishes special indexes and compilations to help you locate quickly the information you need. *The New York Times Biographical Edition* is a compilation of articles from the newspaper about people in the news, obituaries, features on personalities, and other biographical material. The newspaper's *Obituaries*

Index, 1858-1968 facilitates efficient searches of the newspaper for news stories of nearly every prominent world figure and many lesser-known personalities. And do not forget *The New York Times Index* (item 39), which is the master key to the names and activities of persons covered by stories in *The New York Times* newspaper. Most larger libraries will have back issues of the newspaper on microfilm.

News stories and features on personalities published in other newspapers are compiled in bimonthly issues of *Biography News,* a publication of the Gale Research Company. About fifty leading U.S. daily newspapers are tapped for news articles, as well as articles that reflect the essence of personal interviews.

In addition to newspapers, other types of reference books are overlooked frequently as biographical sources. Encyclopedias, for example, are generally the single best source for locating quickly biographical material; and dictionaries (see Chapter 4) and a variety of fact books (see Chapter 5) often include data-type sketches for many significant and even minor personalities.

There are so many special biographical reference books that it would be futile to list more than a few of the more useful in this book. Those listed are among the most widely distributed in libraries. Other important sources are available in many libraries, which identify personalities by profession or vocation, by area of residence or national origin, or according to general prominence whether living or dead. Major publishers of these include: Marquis Who's Who Inc., 200 East Ohio Street, Chicago, Illinois 60611; R.R. Bowker Company, 1180 Avenue of the Americas, New York, New York 10036; The H.W. Wilson Company, 950 University Avenue, Bronx, New York 10452; St. Martin's Press, 175 Fifth Avenue, New York, New York 10010; Gale Research Company, Book Tower, Detroit, Michigan 48226. Write for their catalogs.

INDEXES

There are many timesaving shortcuts and methods that are used in searching biographical sources. Librarians will begin a search by deciding first what is actually required. Do you want brief data, as found in a who's who? Longer sketches? Or perhaps lengthy and critical narrative? Next, is the person in whom you are interested living or dead? Is the person currently newsworthy or historically significant? In all cases your answers will point you to certain types of biographical sources.

Sometimes you already will be familiar with an encyclopedia, fact book, newspaper article, or one of the special biographical dictionaries that will present the information. In most cases you will save time by checking first the *Biographical Dictionaries Master Index* (item 126) in order to learn if a specific source includes the name you are searching. Once you know which reference source you want—or if you draw a blank through the *Biographical Dictionaries Master Index* (item 126)—ask your librarian for assistance! Librarians know where the biographical reference books are located. Or if you do not know what you want they will assist you in searching the references listed in this book as well as in others.

126. *Biographical Dictionaries Master Index*. Detroit, Michigan: Gale Research Company, 1975–1976, updated at two-year intervals. NOTE: Here is the most important timesaver available for searching biographical reference books. Without it you must often search dozens of sources to find a single reference. With it you will reduce searching time in such divers

sources as *Celebrity Register,* the Marquis who's who publications, *Directory of American Scholars, Who's Who in the Theatre,* and about fifty other sources.

127. *Biography Index.* New York: The H.W. Wilson Company, 1946 to date, quarterly with annual and three-year cumulations. NOTE: Use this to locate biographical material (including obituaries), which is published in current books and magazines. It is particularly useful if you need critical or descriptive information about contemporary personalities.

128. Slocum, Robert B., ed. *Biographical Dictionaries and Related Works.* Detroit, Michigan: Gale Research Company, 1967 with 1972 supplement. NOTE: Over 8,170 sources of biographical information are listed in the two volumes of this guide. It includes collections of epitaphs, genealogical works, dictionaries of anonyms and pseudonyms, and other standard references. Sources from all countries and periods are included. The extent of the listings is overwhelming to all but trained librarians. If you must use it, ask for assistance.

BIOGRAPHICAL DICTIONARIES

Biographical dictionaries and other works of collective biography are published to cover people in four main catagories: nationality (specific or universal), vocation, living (current), and deceased (retrospective). Each of the standard references listed below is categorized into one or more of these areas.

129. *American Authors, 1600–1900.* New York: The H.W. Wilson Company, 1938, (retrospective). NOTE: The

sketches of authors vary in length from 150 to 2,500 words. Authors from different periods and countries are included in other titles of H.W. Wilson's "Authors Series": *British Authors Before 1800; British Authors of the Nineteenth Century; European Authors: 1000-1900; The Junior Book of Authors; More Junior Authors; Third Book of Junior Authors; World Authors, 1950-1970* (Item 144); and *Twentieth Century Authors* (item 140). Most of these are edited by Stanley J. Kunitz and Howard Haycraft. For broader, more up-to-date, but less-detailed coverage, use *Contemporary Authors* (item 132).

130. *American Men and Women of Science.* New York: R.R. Bowker Company, (current, American and Canadian). NOTE: Periodic revisions have made this a standard source for brief but essential biographical data. Volumes in the work include those for the physical and biological sciences; social and behavorial sciences; agricultural, animal, and veterinary sciences; economics; medical sciences; and urban community sciences. For longer, more critical essays on scientists, use the *Dictionary of Scientific Biography* (item 135).

131. *Chamber's Biographical Dictionary.* New York: St. Martin's Press, (current, retrospective, universal). NOTE: Most of the figures included are deceased, but *Chamber's* is notable for the extra human-interest information added to each personal data-type entry. It is periodically revised and should be used as a companion with *Webster's Biographical Dictionary* (item 141).

132. *Contemporary Authors.* Detroit, Michigan: Gale Research Company, 1962 to date, (current, retrospective, universal). NOTE: Because of the broad scope of this work, you can learn more about more authors

than from any similar reference work. The Wilson works (item 129) present longer, descriptive articles, but on fewer authors. Only authors whose sole works have been published by a vanity press are excluded by *Contemporary Authors*. Older volumes in the series are regularly revised, updated, and expanded. A "Permanent Series" began in 1975 and compiles sketches from the regular volumes for authors who are no longer publishing or are deceased.

133. *Current Biography*. New York: The H.W. Wilson Company, 1945 to date, monthly except August, yearly cumulation, (current, universal). NOTE: This is the first place to look for excellent articles on the lives of people prominent in the news—in national and international affairs, the sciences, arts, labor, and industry. Includes photographs.

134. *Dictionary of American Biography*. New York: Charles Scribner's Sons, (retrospective, American). NOTE: Usually called the *DAB*, this work is recognized as the authoritative record of the lives of celebrated men and women of America. The basic twenty-volume set is supplemented by new volumes, but there is quite a time-lapse between the death of subjects and their eventual inclusion. You must use *Current Biography* (item 133) or the biographical publications of *The New York Times* (see the introduction to this chapter) in order to fill the gap. The model for the *DAB* is the *Dictionary of National Biography (DNB)*, the classic record of British subjects, which is found with the *DAB* in larger libraries.

135. *Dictionary of Scientific Biography*. New York: Charles Scribner's Sons, (retrospective, universal). NOTE: Patterned after the *DAB* (item 134), this is the major encyclopedic reference set for biographies of people who have contributed to the advancement of sci-

ence. For shorter sketches use *American Men and
Women of Science* (item 130).

136. *Directory of American Scholars*. New York: R.R.
Bowker Company, (current, American). NOTE: Brief
personal data similar to a who's who dictionary is
given for teachers and researchers in all fields. It is
revised periodically. *Leaders in Education* is a similar Bowker reference work. The *National Faculty
Directory*, a related reference work, is published by
the Gale Research Company, but includes only directory information such as names and addresses.

137. *The International Who's Who*. London: Europa Publications Limited, annual, (current, universal). NOTE:
Essential biographical facts about prominent world
personalities are presented in a concise but clear
style.

138. *The McGraw-Hill Encyclopedia of World Biography*.
New York: McGraw-Hill Book Company, 1973, (retrospective, universal). NOTE: The articles for this
twelve-volume work were written for students, and
the set is found most often in school and public
libraries. It is not only a useful teaching aid, but also
an authoritative source. A piece of history is con-
veyed through each biography, and the unique maps,
color plates, and bibliography liven up the data and
commentary.

139. *The National Cyclopedia of American Biography*.
Clifton, New Jersey: James T. White & Company,
(current, retrospective, American). NOTE: A "Permanent Series" of deceased subjects and a "Current
Series" for living subjects present an inclusive,
easy-to-use, and reliable research source. Includes
portraits.

140. *Twentieth Century Authors*. New York: The H.W.
Wilson Company, 1942 with 1955 supplement, (re-

trospective, universal). NOTE: The articles in these two volumes are unique because many authors wrote their own sketches or contributed quotable material. *World Authors, 1950–1970* (item 144) continues this work. Try *Contemporary Authors* (item 132) for more comprehensive inclusion of authors.

141. *Webster's Biographical Dictionary*. Springfield, Massachusetts: G.&C. Merriam Company, (current, retrospective, universal). NOTE: The data given is sketchy, but the work is periodically revised. It is useful for identifying obscure people. Use it also as a companion with *Chamber's Biographical Dictionary* (item 131).

142. *Who's Who*. London: Adam & Charles Black, 1849 to date, annual, (current, British). NOTE: You simply expect to find this classic biographical dictionary in any large library. But do not confuse it with other national versions such as *Who's Who in America* (item 143). A companion publication is *Who Was Who*, which periodically compiles the information on people no longer living and formerly listed in the parent work.

143. *Who's Who in America*. Chicago: Marquis Who's Who, 1899 to date, biennial, (current, American). NOTE: This is the best single source for contemporary American biography. But do not confuse it with *Who's Who* (item 142) or other national biographical dictionaries. The publisher, Marquis Who's Who, also publishes four regional volumes covering notables in the South and Southwest, West, Midwest, and East. If you do not find your subject in *Who's Who in America*, check the regional volumes. A companion publication is *Who Was Who in America*, a compilation of data on eminent people no longer living.

144. *World Authors, 1950–1970.* New York: H.W. Wilson Company, 1975, (current, universal). NOTE: *World Authors* is another addition to the Wilson "Authors Series" (see item 129). It continues *Twentieth Century Authors* (item 140), but with worldwide coverage and more lengthy, critical articles. Inclusion in this work is highly selective. Try *Contemporary Authors* (item 132) for more comprehensive inclusion of authors.

BIOGRAPHICAL DIRECTORIES

A telephone directory or city directory will often provide biographical information. How do you spell a person's name? What is his title? Where does he live? Special directories are also available that do much the same thing. Examples are the *Federal Directory* (formerly called the *Federal Telephone Directory*), *The National Faculty Directory,* and the membership directories of organizations and professional associations.

State legislative directories, or "bluebooks," are published by many states as guides to the people and activities of state government. These are further described in the "State Government Publications" section of Chapter 10 in this book.

Special problems are posed by the organization of the U.S. Congress. But they are solvable by using two indispensable directories found in most libraries.

145. *Congressional Staff Directory.* Alexandria, Virginia: The Congressional Staff Directory, 1959 to date, annual. NOTE: Here is your guidebook to the Congressional bureaucracy puzzle. In addition to the hundreds of biographies of key staff members, you can

put your finger on names, addresses, positions, organizations, assignments, and other information unavailable in any other convenient compilation. Notice that this is not an official government publication. The *Official Congressional Directory* (item 146) is the authorized source, but it does not serve the same purpose and must be used as a companion reference.

146. *Official Congressional Directory*. Washington, D.C.: U.S. Government Printing Office, 1809 to date, annual. NOTE: Biographical sketches for senators, congressmen, and federal judges make up a major part of this. But the most valuable sections include listings of personnel of all government agencies and departments, foreign representatives, and members of the Washington, D.C. Press Corps. There is also a section of maps of congressional districts. You may find the *Almanac of American Politics* (item 110) more convenient to use for some information. Also use the *Congressional Staff Directory* (item 145) as a companion reference. For a retrospective source of congressional biography, use an encyclopedia or ask your librarian for the *Biographical Directory of the American Congress, 1774–1961*. For a record of congressional activity see the official *Congressional Record* and its *Index* (item 170). A more convenient summary record is found in *Congress and the Nation* (item 113), the *Congressional Quarterly Almanac* (item 114), and *CQ Weekly Report* (item 180). For a description of federal government organization see the *United States Government Manual* (item 124). Use the *Washington Information Directory* (item 202) to locate the best sources of information in Washington, D.C.

7. Quotations

The best books of quotations are those that give you the material you need. That may sound facetious until you consider the divers sources of quotations: ballads, the *Bible*, proverbs, maxims, speeches, uncounted numbers of books and articles, and more. Every word uttered or written is a potential quotation, and no single source will verify or identify all the particular quotations you want. Naturally some quotations are duplicated from one reference book to another, but each book is unique in at least some of its content.

The Bartlett and Stevenson works listed in this chapter are the most famous quote books. But new books are always being published. To learn what they are check *Subject Guide to Books in Print* (item 55) or *Subject Guide to Forthcoming Books* (item 67). Libraries tend to buy as many different quotation sources as budgets will allow. Ask for the location of these references or look in the library's card catalog under "Quotations" for specific quote books that the library owns.

Searching quotations can be time consuming. Your librarian will help you find quotable material on a subject, or will track down the source of a quotation if it is to be found.

147. Bartlett, John. *Familiar Quotations*. Boston: Little, Brown and Company. NOTE: Each revision of Bartlett is arranged chronologically by author, which is usually a nuisance unless you use the author index or the excellent main index. The latter is a voluminous key-word index that occupies fully one-third of the volume. Footnotes and cross-references give you other keys to tracing the history and origin of quotations.

148. Stevenson, Burton. *Home Book of Quotations, Classical and Modern*. New York: Dodd, Mead & Company. NOTE: Periodic revisions and the sheer size of this work make it a popular, comprehensive work. It is arranged by subject, but includes an index of authors and a lengthy key-word index. Stevenson was also the compiler of other notable quotation reference books. Among them are: *The Home Book of Bible Quotations; The Home Book of Proverbs, Maxims and Familiar Phrases;* and *The Standard Book of Shakespeare Quotations*.

8. Statistics

Statistics these days are used in an attempt to prove or disprove almost everything. They are used in a variety of areas including sports, TV ratings, population trends, the stock market. It is hard to imagine anything not described by statistics; and by their very nature, statistics give the impression of great value and accuracy. But how often is your search for statistics frustrated or even given up as a fruitless task? How do you know when you have reliable statistics? Or even the best statistics available?

In most cases the best single source for statistics is the U.S. Government. "Official Government statistics," in fact, vie for our attention every day in such forms as data on wages and salaries, unemployment figures, and the consumer and wholesale price indexes. Such figures are creditable, but they are subject to inaccuracies and limitations. For example, just compiling all the statistics generated by the U.S. Government for publication is bound to result in some imperfections. Statistics also can be extremely misleading because of the way they are reported, interpreted, or utilized. Nevertheless, the Congress, executive agencies, and many bureaus all produce statistical publications. They are easy to locate through the essential *American Statistics*

Index (item 150); or just being familiar with a few major sources will result in your ability to find most statistics you need.

The major U.S. Government source for statistics is the Bureau of the Census, which collects large amounts of data on many measures of American life. The bureau not only publishes detailed census reports, but also issues guides to its publications and indispensable summaries such as the *Statistical Abstract of the United States* (item 154). Write for a free catalog of publications from the Director, Bureau of the Census, Washington, D.C. 20233.

Other U.S. Government agencies also publish major statistical material. The U.S. Department of Labor issues the *Monthly Labor Review*. The Federal Reserve Board publishes the monthly *Federal Reserve Bulletin*. The Treasury Department issues a monthly *Treasury Bulletin*. And the Social Security Administration publishes a monthly *Social Security Bulletin*. Each provide current data on significant issues and areas of concern.

The U.S. Department of Commerce publishes the *Survey of Current Business*, an invaluable monthly publication of business and economic statistics. The data and analysis reported in each monthly issue is supplemented by weekly statistical summaries. *Business Statistics* is issued biennially as an historical supplement with detailed notes and exact source references.

In addition to the statistical reports of the U.S. Government, statistics are included in encyclopedias and many fact books such as the almanacs, handbooks, and yearbooks listed in Chapter 5. Other reference books that include significant statistics are the *Rand McNally Commerical Atlas and Marketing Guide* (item 160) and the *Editor & Publisher Marketing Guide* a companion volume to the *Editor & Publisher International Year Book* (item 213).

If you need current statistics, keep in mind such indexes as

Business Periodicals Index (item 24), *Public Affairs Infor-mation Service Bulletin* (item 31), *The New York Times Index* (item 39), and *The Wall Street Journal Index* (item 40). They will lead you to statistics published in current magazines and other topical sources.

If you cannot put your finger on the precise statistics you need, ask your librarian for assistance. A librarian can simp-lify significantly your search for statistical information.

149. *America Votes*. Washington, D.C.: Congressional Quarterly Service. NOTE: Each new volume in this series details the results of the immediate-past na-tional election, including gubernatorial races. Vote totals, percentages, pluralities by county in each state and by ward in larger cities are tallied. Maps supplement the statistics. Congressional Quarterly is also the publisher of two related reference books: the *Guide to U.S. Elections,* an historical collection of election returns, and *Presidential Elections Since 1789.*

150. *American Statistics Index: A Comprehensive Guide and Index to the Statistical Publications of the United States Government*. Washington, D.C.: Congressional Information Service, 1973 to date, annual with monthly updating supplements. NOTE: No matter what the field of interest, use this as your first step in finding statistical publications on Ameri-can issues as well as matters of worldwide concern. Commonly called *ASI,* it is much more than an index. Statistical publications are indexed in the first part of *ASI,* and then abstracted in the second volume. The abstracts are exceptional research aids in them-selves. In addition to giving detailed information about the publications, each includes references to related material.

151. *The Gallup Opinion Index; political, social and*

economic trends. Princeton, New Jersey: The American Institute of Public Opinion, 1965 to date, monthly. NOTE: Each issue reports on the results of Gallup surveys that have been conducted nationally on various aspects of American life. A fascinating companion to this is *The Gallup Poll; Public Opinion, 1935–1971,* published in three volumes by Random House. It is a compilation of every Gallup Poll issued by the American Institute of Public Opinion for the period.

152. *Survey of Buying Power*. New York: Sales Management, 1960 to date, annual. NOTE: This is published specifically as a business marketing guide. But it is generally the most useful compilation of data available on population estimates, income, and retail sales. The figures, drawn from U.S. Bureau of the Census reports, are rearranged conveniently by states, cities, metropolitan areas, and even age groups. *Sales Management* magazine also publishes several other important marketing surveys. *Survey of Buying Power, Part II,* is issued annually and presents population projections, income data, and retail sales statistics for the media markets of radio, TV, and newspapers. *The Survey of Industrial Purchasing Power* is published annually and provides data on prime industrial markets.

153. *Statistical Yearbook*. New York: United Nations Department of Economic and Social Affairs, Statistical Office, 1949 to date, annual. NOTE: This is designed as a convenient summary volume of international statistics. It is supplemented by the U.N. *Monthly Bulletin of Statistics*. In addition, a full range of U.N. statistics on specific fields is issued in a series of interrelated reference publications, including the *Demographic Yearbook,* the *Yearbook of National*

Accounts Statistics, Yearbook of International Trade Statistics, and the *Yearbook of Labour Statistics.* Ask your librarian for the location of these sources, or write for further information to: Publishing Service, United Nations, New York, New York 10017.

154. U.S. Bureau of the Census. *Statistical Abstract of the United States.* Washington, D.C.: Government Printing Office, 1878 to date, annual. NOTE: The *Statistical Abstract* is the single most useful volume of summary figures on social, political, economic, and even cultural activities. Further research is made easy because the source of the figures displayed in each chart or table is given. The bureau also publishes other summary statistics in the *County and City Data Book, Historical Statistics of the United States,* and *Congressional District Data Book.*

155. Wasserman, Paul, ed. *Statistics Sources.* Detroit, Michigan: Gale Research Company. NOTE: Although not as detailed and informative as the *American Statistics Index* (item 150), this periodically revised subject guide includes references to statistical publications available from governmental as well as nongovernmental sources. It includes many international references. A very convenient "Selected Bibliography of Key Statistical Sources" is located at the front of the volume.

9. Maps or Geographical Information

Most people have consulted a roadmap at some time for getting from one place to another. If you have never used a map for any other purpose, however, you have missed information gathering at one of its most exciting and imaginative levels.

The symbols, lines, colors, and forms on maps are the most convenient way to visualize the location of places and landmarks. For example, special maps provide comprehensive information of elevations of the land, heights of natural terrain, the inclination of mountain roads, and the extent of populated areas. Some maps illustrate weather patterns, temperature variations, agricultural areas, and the range of vegetation cover. Still others depict international boundaries and the historical movements of civilization.

Accurate maps are designed and drawn to a "scale," which gives the ratio of map distance to ground distance. In addition, there are different types of maps. Common oil company maps are generally planimetric, depicting only the location of roads, cities, and major landmarks. Topographic maps portray manmade and natural features by location as well as in a measurable form as represented by contour lines. Plastic relief maps are topographic maps in a three-dimensional form so you can readily see variation in elevation. Photomaps are reproductions of aerial photographs or a mosaic made from a series of aerial photgraphs. There are also special aeronautical and maritime charts, weather maps, thematic maps, and globes.

A good explanation of how to read and use these various maps is found in the *World Book Encyclopedia* (item 7); or look in most other general encyclopedias as well as the atlases listed in this chapter.

General encyclopedias are also excellent places to look for maps. In addition, the narrative material they include about cities, states, and countries is generally more convenient and in adequate detail for basic information needs. Several of the fact books listed in Chapter 5 also include maps and geographical information.

Libraries will have these general reference books as well as general reference atlases. In many cases you must be resourceful and turn elsewhere to find special maps to meet your particular needs.

TRAVEL GUIDES AND OIL COMPANY MAPS

Use travel guides whether you are taking to the open road or staying put as an armchair tourist. In addition to the numerous maps and photographs, the guidebooks include interesting, readable material on cities, countries, and regions. Standard travel information on transportation, restaurants, and lodging generally is supplemented by descriptions of festivals, sports facilities, famous landmarks, and other sightseeing attractions. The better travel guides are frequently revised and libraries will seldom have the latest edition of the exact guide you want. So turn to your local bookstore or order travel guides direct from a publisher. Your librarian will help you pinpoint the guides that are

available. For example, the popular Fodor's travel guides
are published by the David McKay Company which has
included its catalog in *Publishers' Trade List Annual* (item
68).

Some of the best travel maps and local area descriptions
are available from chambers of commerce or tourist
bureaus. Locate an address or telephone number for these
through a telephone directory. Most research libraries have
a selection of telephone directories from all over the United
States; or, write for directory information to:

Chamber of Commerce of the U.S.A.
1615 H Street, N.W.
Washington, D.C. 20036

Nearly every major oil company service station offers free
road maps; or, you can ask the attendant for an address to
which you can write for information. Oil company maps are
useless, however, if you want to know about an area in
detail. Things such as terrain, elevations, and exact road
routes just do not show up. It is almost impossible to visualize what an area is really like without better maps.

UNITED STATES GOVERNMENT MAPS

The reliable topographic detail on United State Geological
Survey (USGS) maps is unequalled for showing the exact
locations of natural and manmade features on the earth.
USGS maps are available in some libraries. They also may
be purchased from many outdoor recreation shops or from
local USGS offices. Or write for information on maps east of
the Mississippi to:

U.S. Geological Survey
Washington Distribution Section
1200 South Eads Street
Arlington, Virginia 22202

For maps west of the Mississippi write to:
> U.S. Geological Survey
> Distribution Section
> Federal Center
> Denver, Colorado 80225

Beautiful, detailed maps of the U.S. National Forests are available from district Forest Service offices. Or you can write for information to:
> Division of Information and Education
> Forest Service
> Department of Agriculture
> Washington, D.C. 20250

The National Oceanic and Atmospheric Administration (formerly two agencies called the Weather Bureau and the Coast and Geodetic Survey) issues charts of coastal areas, harbors, and rivers, as well as National Weather Service maps. For further information write to:
> Office of Public Affairs
> National Oceanic and Atmospheric
>   Administration
> Department of Commerce
> Rockville, Maryland 20852

In addition to the Geological Survey office in the Department of the Interior, the National Park Service issues maps and other interpretive geographical and environmental material. Write for information to:
> Office of Information
> National Park Service
> Interior Building
> Washington, D.C. 20240

Map information on the vast river systems under the development of the Tennessee Valley Authority (TVA) is available from two outlets:

Maps and Surveys Branch
TVA
200 Haney Building
Chattanooga, Tennessee 37401; or

Maps and Engineering Records Office
TVA
416 Union Avenue
Room 102 Union Building Annex
Knoxville, Tennessee 37902

As an indication of the many other U.S. Government sources for geographical material, more than eighty different agencies supplied information for *The National Atlas of the United States of America* (item 164). Look in the *United States Government Manual* (item 124) for descriptions and addresses of these agencies. Check the *Monthly Catalog* (item 174) for specific maps and other geographical material produced by various agencies and available from the U.S. Government Printing Office.

LOCAL GOVERNMENT MAPS

Many state, city, and county highway or transportation departments issue exceptionally valuable maps that detail exact roadway mileage and locations of significant natural and manmade landmarks. They are designed for surveyors, engineers, and planners, and only larger libraries will collect them. If your library does not have a collection, check a telephone directory and call the road department in your area to confirm the availability and recency of obtainable maps.

UNITED NATIONS MAPS

Another "governmental" source of mapping is the United

Nations and the system of interrelated international organizations. For example, UNESCO produces a series of scientific maps and atlases. Write for free descriptive catalogs and price lists of all available United Nations material to:

UNIPUB, Inc.
Box 433, Murray Hill Station
New York, New York 10016

ATLASES

An atlas is simply a collection of maps bound into a single volume. Atlases tend to become outdated as better and more detailed maps become available. Frequently, however, even new maps cannot keep up with changing national boundaries, the organization of new states, and the natural and manmade changes constantly occurring on the earth's surface. But an atlas is a convenient source to use and they are generally available in libraries. Quickly locate maps in an atlas by turning first to the index, located usually at the back of the volume.

For most geographical questions the atlases listed in this chapter will give the answers. Additional atlases may be identified by looking in *General World Atlases in Print: A Comparative Analysis*, edited by S. Padraig Walsh and published regularly in revised editions by the R.R. Bowker Company.

Ask your librarian for assistance in locating special atlases or unusual geographical information.

156. *Goode's World Atlas*. Chicago: Rand McNally & Company. NOTE: Although designed for school use, *Goode's* is favored as a basic geographic reference book. It is revised frequently and includes multicolored maps of land and ocean floor areas, as well as

several special sections of useful geographic terms, names, and other data.

157. *Hammond Medallion World Atlas*. Maplewood, New Jersey: Hammond Inc. NOTE: Hammond also publishes the *Ambassador World Atlas* and the *Hallmark World Atlas*. All three are basically the same publications but they are designed to sell in different markets. The *Hallmark* is published in two volumes with slipcases and costs more than either of the other two. The *Ambassador* costs the least, but excludes several sections of encyclopedic information included in the *Medallion* and the *Hallmark*. The Ambassador is generally adequate for most uses.

158. *The International Atlas*. Chicago: Rand McNally & Company. NOTE: Serious researchers acclaim this atlas as the best ever produced by an American publisher. Detailed, shaded relief maps cover all land areas of the world. Most of the text is in four languages: English, French, German, and Spanish. The index includes some 160,000 entries. Less scholarly atlases are easier to use for general reference work. Try *Goode's World Atlas* (item 156) or the *Hammond Medallion World Atlas* (item 157). If *The International Atlas* is unavailable, look for the *Britannica Atlas*. The maps in each are identical.

159. *National Geographic Atlas of the World*. Washington, D.C.: The National Geographic Society. NOTE: As with other National Geographic Society publications, their atlas is attractive and informative as well as accurate. Impressive inset maps, mapping detail, and other special features and text set this atlas apart from all others. New editions appear at intervals to keep it up-to-date. In addition to the atlas, many libraries collect the maps that are issued periodically with the monthly *National Geographic* magazine.

Collect these maps personally for a convenient file close at hand.

160. *Rand McNally Commercial Atlas and Marketing Guide*. Chicago: Rand McNally & Company, annual. NOTE: Extensive business and Commercial data supplements maps for each state in the United States. Maps of Canada and other countries are included, but the emphasis is on the United States. In addition, numerous special maps depict road and railway routes, population characteristics, retail and manufacturing areas, and other significant data of commercial interest.

161. *Rand McNally Road Atlas*. Chicago: Rand McNally & Company, annual. NOTE: When traveling across state boundaries or international borders, a road atlas is a convenient reference book to have along. The colorful *Rand McNally Road Atlas* covers the U.S., Canada, Mexico, and has been a familiar favorite with travelers for over fifty years. It is also a convenient, practical supplement to the *Rand McNally Commercial Atlas and Marketing Guide* (item 160). Rand McNally publishes other travel guides. Write for a list to:

> Rand McNally & Company
> P.O. Box 7600
> Chicago, Illinois 60680

Road atlases from other publishers are sometimes available in libraries and almost always wherever books and magazines are sold.

162. Shepherd, William R. *Historical Atlas*. New York: Barnes & Noble. NOTE: The history of civilization from Ancient Egypt to modern times is covered in this respected general historical atlas. Reprinted editions with supplemental additions are published periodically. Other historical atlases include the

Oxford Bible Atlas; the U.S. Military Academy's *The West Point Atlas of American Wars; The American Heritage Pictorial Atlas of United States History;* and the *Atlas of American History* by James Truslow Adams. Ask your librarian for additional historical atlases covering certain time periods, countries, and subjects.

163. *The Times Atlas of the World.* Comprehensive Edition. London: Times Newspapers Limited. NOTE: This frequently revised geographical reference book is the most exhaustive, scholarly atlas available. In addition, the maps are strikingly beautiful. There are also inset maps, and the work is extensively indexed. Because of the cost many libraries may not have this significant atlas. So look for *The New York Times World Atlas,* a smaller atlas patterned after *The Times Atlas of the World.*

164. U.S. Geological Survey. *The National Atlas of the United States of America.* Washington, D.C.: Government Printing Office. NOTE: The first part of *The National Atlas* is devoted to general reference maps. Special thematic maps make up the majority of the atlas. They relate statistical data to places, illustrate American historical development, and depict the physical, economic, social, political, and cultural characteristics of the nation.

165. *World Book Atlas.* Chicago: Field Enterprise Educational Corporation. NOTE: This is a widely accepted supplement to the *World Book Encyclopedia* (item 7). Even though it is designed for young people, the material is generally adequate for basic geographical research. Another notable atlas published as a companion to an encyclopedia is the *Britannica Atlas.* The maps in the *Britannica Atlas* are exactly the same as those in *The International Atlas.* (item 158).

GAZETTEERS

Gazetteers are geographical name dictionaries or guides to place names. An index at the back of an atlas is a type of gazetteer, although it does not give descriptive definitions.

As an alternative to gazetteers, check a dictionary or encyclopedia. General dictionaries include brief descriptions of geographical features. Encyclopedias generally include far greater detail than does a gazetteer for the names they commonly include. Gazetteers, however, pick up many obscure place names and geographical features overlooked by other reference books.

166. *The Columbia Lippincott Gazetteer of the World*. New York: Columbia University Press, 1962. NOTE: About 130,000 places and geographic features are described in considerable detail. The work is dated but excellent for the period it covers.

167. *Webster's New Geographical Dictionary*. Springfield, Massachusetts: G.&C. Merriam Company, 1972. NOTE: This reference book is convenient to use, but it includes the pertinent facts for fewer than 48,000 entries. *The Columbia Lippincott Gazetteer of the World* (item 166) is dated but far more comprehensive. Other gazetteers may be required to complete your research. Ask your librarian for assistance.

10. Government Publications

There is an incredible range of government publications from sources as diverse as the United States Government, foreign governments, the United Nations and related agencies, as well as from other international governmental organizations. Because these publications are frequently difficult to locate they are all too often thought of as something unique and mysterious. Actually their purpose is no different from materials issued by commercial publishers. They are published to be informative—even entertaining.

Governments frequently issue some of the most colorful and attractive publications available. For example, the outstanding *The National Atlas of the United States of America* (item 164) was produced by the U.S. Geological Survey. Beautiful scientific maps and atlases are also available from the United Nations. Then there are the irreplaceable compilations of statistics and other data. *The Statistical Abstract of the United States* (item 154), which is itself based on myriad government statistical reports, and the United Nations *Statistical Yearbook* (item 153) are examples.

Most government publications, however, are not reference books. They are practical materials aimed at consumers, teachers, business people, scientists, scholars, and anyone else who may need them. The formats of these publications include books, magazines, pamphlets, reports, maps, atlases, microforms, and an array of miscellaneous documents.

In order to locate these materials you must rely on a number of special indexes and bibliographic guides. Where they are not available you may sometimes locate the material you need through the *Public Affairs Information Service Bulletin* (item 31). It is invaluable for identifying many United States and United Nations documents. Some state and municipal documents are also included. Most research, however, must be carried out by utilizing the guides listed in this chapter. If you cannot find what you want through the basic references, ask a librarian for assistance! Unless you regularly search out and use government publications, you will seldom have time to discover for yourself just what is available and how and where it is organized.

U.S. GOVERNMENT PUBLICATIONS

The U.S. Government is the most prolific publisher in the world. Material is produced from most agencies in the legislative, executive, and judicial branches, and it covers virtually every subject and in every conceivable format. Unfortunately, most of it never appears in the majority of libraries. Even libraries that are designated as U.S. Government documents depositories will acquire only about half of the total available. Depository libraries receive Government Printing Office (GPO) publications free of charge from the Superintendent of Documents. If you are fortunate to live near one of these libraries, you have the right as a citizen to use any of the GPO publications held by that library. Publications issued from agencies other than the GPO may not be available.

Keep up with GPO publications by checking regularly the *Monthly Catalog of United States Government Publications* (item 174) available in most larger libraries; or personally receive the biweekly *Selected List of U.S. Government Publications*. It lists new materials of popular interest for sale by the GPO and may be obtained free upon request to:

> Superintendent of Documents
> U.S. Government Printing Office
> Washington, D.C. 20402

Check the *Guide to U.S. Government Publications* (item 171) to learn what publications are issued by all the various government agencies. Look in the *United States Government Manual* (item 124) for descriptions and addresses of agencies other than the GPO, which distribute published material.

In some libraries U.S. Government publications are listed in the card catalog and treated like any other library material. In many places the publications are maintained separately and you must rely on a number of special guides in order to identify available materials. Several are listed in this chapter. In addition, the *American Statistics Index* (item 150) is the principal aid for locating government statistical documents.

Only the basic guides and indexes are listed in this book, and for most research the use of a few will be adequate. These are the *Monthly Catalog of United States Government Publications* (item 173), the *American Statistics Index* (item150), and the *Congressional Information Service/Index* (item 168). There are many more research aids available, but unless you use government publications regularly, rely on your librarian for additional assistance.

168. *Congressional Information Service / Index*. Washington, D.C.: Congessional Information Service, monthly with annual volumes. NOTE:

Commonly called the *CIS/Index,* this vital reference
work indexes nearly all U.S. Congressional publications. It does not cover the *Congressional Record,*
which has its own *Index* (item 169); nor does it cover
reports and hearings on private bills, reports dealing
with matters of Congressional "housekeeping," or
documents reprinted from previous publications.
The *CIS/Index* is particularly valuable for its inclusion of legislative histories in the annual volumes.
Congressional Information Service also issues a microfiche collection of the documentation indexed.
This collection may be available in larger libraries. A
similar reference service to the *CIS/Index* is the
Congressional Index published by Commerce Clear-
ing House.

169. *Congressional Record Index.* Washington, D.C.: Government Printing Office, biweekly with annual cumulation. NOTE: The *Congressional Record* is the daily
record of the proceedings of Congress. It reports the
speeches and actions that have occurred, as well as
much that is inserted by members of Congress as
"extensions" of their remarks. The *Index* metic-
ulously cites this record of information by name and
subject. A more convenient summary of congressional activity is found in *Congress and the Nation*
(item 113), the *Congressional Quarterly Almanac*
(item 114), and *CQ Weekly Report* (item 179). Check
the *Official Congressional Directory* (item 146) and
the *Congressional Staff Directory* (item 145) for a
record of who's who in the U.S. Congress. Look in
the *United States Code* for a record of the laws
passed by Congress.

170. *Guide to U.S. Government Publications.* McLean,
Virginia: Documents Index, updating looseleaf service. NOTE: Check this list when you want to know

what publications are issued by the various government agencies. Volume one covers the publications of current agencies, while volume two covers the publications once issued by abolished agencies. A cumulative, paperbound index to the two looseleaf volumes is issued periodically.

171. *Cumulative Subject Guide to U.S. Government Bibliographies 1924–1973*. Washington, D.C.: Carrollton Press. NOTE: More than 40,000 bibliographies are listed. Fewer than five percent are listed in *Bibliographic Index* (item 53). An annual updating service keeps the basic seven-volume set current. Carrollton Press also issues a microfiche collection of the documentation indexed. This collection may be available in larger libraries.

172. *Index to U.S. Government Periodicals*. Chicago: Infordata International Inc., 1974 to date, quarterly with annual cumulations. NOTE: Before this index, there was never an exclusive indexing service to government magazines or periodicals. This is a very important computer-generated author and subject guide to selected magazines. Unfortunately the number of titles represented is a minority of the total available.

173. *Monthly Catalog of United States Government Publications*. Washington, D.C.: Superintendent of Documents, monthly. NOTE: The *Monthly Catalog* is the principal key to the use of goverment publications. It includes complete bibliographic citations, information on how to locate documents, and instructions for ordering them. There is an annual cumulative index. There is also *The Cumulative Subject Index to the Monthly Catalog of U.S. Government Publications, 1900–1971* published by Carrollton Press. Only large research libraries will have *The*

Cumulative Subject Index. A useful self-help guide to the *Monthly Catalog* is *The Monthly Catalog of United States Government Publications: An Introduction to its Use,* written by John Gordon Burke and Carol Dugan Wilson and published by Linnet Books.

174. Morehead, Joe. *Introduction to United States Public Documents.* Littleton, Colorado: Libraries Unlimited, 1975. NOTE: This is a textbook that is also useful as a self-help guide. It includes many illustrations and a detailed index. An older but still useful guide is *Government Publications and Their Use,* written by Laurence F. Schmeckebier and Roy R. Eastin and published by The Brookings Institution.

175. Wynkoop, Sally. *Government Reference Books: A Biennial Guide to U.S. Government Publications.* Littleton, Colorado: Libraries Unlimited. NOTE: This is an annotated guide to bibliographies, directories, indexes, dictionaries, statistical works, handbooks, almanacs, catalogs, and biographical directories. Libraries Unlimited also publishes *Subject Guide to Goverment Reference Books* and *A Guide to Popular Government Publications: For Libraries and Home Reference.*

STATE GOVERNMENT PUBLICATIONS

You must be very resourceful in tracking down state government publications. There are few indexes, guides, or checklists in the field, and libraries generally do not collect state or local publications from places other than the home state or local area. They are too difficult to identify and acquire. They tend to be illusive even after they are published.

For these reasons, most librarians generally are not very helpful in this area, particularly if the library does not have the few bibliographic research guides on hand. An inquiry to a state agency for specific information will frequently get the best results. Inquiries to state libraries by correspondence or telephone may also net results in locating specific reference material. Your librarian will help you locate the name and address of the agency or library you need.

In order to locate the right state government office, your librarian may turn to a telephone directory or a state legislative manual commonly known as a "bluebook." These bluebooks are guides to a wealth of information not found elsewhere concerning the workings of state governments. You will find in them lists and biographical material on appointed and elected officials. Legislative information, material about voting districts, and statistical data from census figures, voting records, and election results are included. Functions and organization of administrative, judicial, and legislative agencies are detailed. And much more. Ask your librarian for bluebooks to specific states.

176. Hernon, Peter. "State Publications: A Bibliographic Guide for Reference Collections." *Library Journal*, volume 99 (November 1, 1974), pp. 2810-2819. NOTE: Mr. Hernon is a reference librarian who has wrestled with the problems of state government publications for several years. His guide has been updated and expanded from an earlier one published in 1972. In addition to the list of publications having general reference value, he identifies other checklists such as the Library of Congress *Monthly Checklist of State Publications* and the Council of State Governments' Legislative Research Checklist.

177. Parish, David W. *State Government Reference Publications: An Annotated Bibliography*. Littleton, Col-

orado: Libraries Unlimited, 1974. NOTE: More than eight-hundred important and representative documents issued by various state agencies are listed and annotated. Appendices include a bibliography of other books and articles about the field and a directory of agencies represented in the main part of the book.

UNITED NATIONS PUBLICATIONS

The United Nations, including the interrelated agencies such as UNESCO, is publishing an ever-increasing amount of quality material. It is coming in all formats and on divers subjects. All of it is available in English, and much of it is firmly established as essential for research. An example is the *Statistical Yearbook* (item 153).

United Nations publications available in libraries are generally listed in the card catalog and treated as is other library material. Or write for free catalogs and price lists to:

       UNIPUB, Inc.
       Box 433, Murray Hill Station
       New York, New York 10016

178. Winton, Harry N.M. *Publications of the United Nations System: A Reference Guide*. New York: R.R. Bowker Company, 1972. NOTE: Hundreds of reference works and magazines issued by the U.N. are listed and annnotated. Three main sections cover general U.N. information including addresses, subjects of publications, lists of catalogs, indexes, and bibliographies; major reference publications; and magazines. The book is published jointly by R.R. Bowker and UNIPUB.

OTHER INTERNATIONAL ORGANIZATIONS

Check *The Statesman's Year-Book* (item 123) for a list of international organizations. Each listing includes a description of the organization, an address, and a list of publications issued by the organization.

11. Perspective on the News

Where do you find concise, factual summaries of yesterday's newsworthy events, developments, and circumstances? The task can be extremely difficult if you try to locate convenient material on the news of last week or last year in newspapers, newsmagazines or books. They just are not designed to help you quickly find the information you need when you need it. For quick answers to current events questions you must look in special news digests, which gather, summarize, organize, and index essential news material.

The New York Times Index (item 39) is the best single source that will help you put your finger on specific newsworthy facts and data. On the other hand, do not overlook the essential digests that summarize the news from additional newspapers, magazines, broadcasts, and other news sources. They are up-to-date encyclopedias of news events and are frequently indispensable sources for easily tracing events or identifying facts, figures, and other data.

179. *CQ Weekly Report.* Washington, D.C.: Congressional Quarterly, Inc., 1943 to date, weekly with quarterly cumulating indexes. NOTE: Here is the most con-

venient digest of information on U.S. Congressional activities. It includes commentary on major issues, reports on committee activities, records of floor action, and charts showing the progress and status of major legislation. The annual *Congressional Quarterly Almanac* (item 114) further summarizes the material from *CQ Weekly Report*. Check the *Congressional Record* with its *Index* (item 169) for an official daily record of Congressional proceedings. Look in the *Official Congressional Directory* (item 146) for material describing the personalities and organization of the U.S. Congress.

180. *Editorials on File*. New York: Facts on File, 1970 to date, twice monthly with monthly and quarterly cumulative indexes. NOTE: Each issue reprints a selection of newspaper editorials that profile the controversies and debate the issues that make up the news. Editorials from U.S. and Canadian newspapers are organized according to subject. Each subject is introduced by a brief factual summary of background events. A related publication is *Editorial Research Reports* (item 181).

181. *Editorial Research Reports*. Washington, D.C.: Congressional Quarterly, Inc. 1965 to date, weekly with semiannual cumulations. NOTE: Each report analyzes an important issue currently receiving public attention. The reports include current and historical background, pro and con assessment, and bibliographies for further study. Another publication devoted to assessing controversial topics of national importance is *The Congressional Digest*. This monthly magazine includes factual background material and pro and con analysis of the topics.

182. *Facts on File*. New York: Facts on File, 1941 to date, weekly with twice monthly cumulative indexes and

annual yearbooks. NOTE: Each issue summarizes material from news sources around the world to give researchers a convenient, accessible record of basic information on countless topics. *Keesing's Contemporary Archives,* the British counterpart, reports more fully on topics than does *Facts on File*. Other news digests in the style of *Keesing's Contemporary Archives* are the *Asian Recorder* and the *African Recorder*.

12. Other Sources of Information: Directories

There are thousands of sources other than your favorite library from which materials may be borrowed or information requested. The *Guide to American Directories* (item 194) lists over five-thousand directories that, in turn, may help you identify an unbelievable range of these sources.

For most purposes go directly to the major source guides listed in this chapter as well as the next. One of the most popular directories, for example, is the *Encyclopedia of Associations* (item 190). It will tell you exactly whom to write, phone, or visit in an association for the latest facts, figures, and opinions on nearly every area of human activity. Or, try the "Market Place" directories published by the R.R. Bowker Company and listed in the next chapter. The *Literary Market Place* (item 218), *Fine Arts Market Place* (item 213), *Photography Market Place* (item 221), and others, present listings for all the people, companies, and services you need when buying or selling in the areas.

There is also a multitude of special libraries and special collections within general libraries. These are listed in the *Directory of Special Libraries and Information Centers* (item 188) and *Subject Collections* (item 199). In selecting one of these libraries for your purposes, remember that the size and diversity of a library's holdings are less important than the availability of specific information you need when you need it. Even the largest academic or public research libraries will not have all the right material for every writing project. Some of the best libraries are small and tucked away in the most inconspicuous places. They may be just around the corner, up the street, across town, or convenient to you through the mail or your library's interlibrary loan service (item 236). They are frequently overlooked. Survey your local library resources and there is a good chance you will find one that will serve your needs better than the library you are now utilizing.

For example, school libraries or the children's section in a public library may be the best place to start looking for general background information. Or special libraries—and special librarians—are unusually helpful for specific research projects. Among these, commercial or corporation libraries are nearly always the best place to find the latest information in a particular business field. Other special libraries are maintained to meet the information needs of authoritative groups such as private research organizations, historical and genealogical societies, community agencies, museums, and professional associations. Most of them are also open to other researchers.

Government agencies support numerous libraries, information centers, and even bookstores. The U.S. Government, for example, is an endless source of information. Just check the *United States Government Manual* (item 124), the *Washington Information Directory* (item 201), or *A Directory of Information Resources in the United States* (item 187).

State and local government information offices are more difficult to identify. You will save time by going directly to specific government agency offices with your questions. Or, ask your librarian for assistance in identifying which agencies will most likely have the material you need. A telephone directory is usually your best guide.

Finally, a visit to your local bookstore may be useful to your research. Find out where they are located by checking the yellow pages in a telephone directory. Next to your librarian and the specialists who work in information centers and special libraries, an experienced, knowlegeable bookseller can identify quickly the newest books for you. Other book dealers will be your best source for used or rare books, old magazines, and many other manuscripts and documents. In addition, a bookstore may be the most convenient place for you to find and use the basic book trade catalogs such as *Books In Print* (item 54), *Subject Guide to Books in Print* (item 55) and *Paperbound Books in Print* (item 57).

183. *American Library Directory*. New York: R.R. Bowker Company, biennial. NOTE: Complete directory listings for public libraries, academic libraries, and special libraries are arranged alphabetically by state and city. You can easily locate addresses and telephone numbers, as well as names of key personnel. In addition, data on the size of a library and its special collections is also included. For a list of special libraries check the *Directory of Special Libraries and Information Centers* (item 188). Look in *Subject Collections* (item 199) for lists of special collections of material within libraries.

184. Carroll, John M. *Confidential Information Sources: Public & Private*. Los Angeles, California: Security World Books, 1975. NOTE: Here is a unique behind-the-scenes guide to confidential personal information in public and private records. It reveals what information is on file, how it is gathered, what it is used for, who uses it, where it is available, and who

has access to it.

185. *Consultants and Counsulting Organizations Directory*.
Detroit, Michigan: Gale Research Company. NOTE:
Find out who and where the experts are for
thousands of fields. Each reference includes the
name, address, and telephone number of an organization, plus a description of services and types of
consulting performed. *Who's Who in Consulting* is
also published by Gale Research Company. It is a
guide to professional personnel engaged in consulta-
tion for business, industry, and government. *New
Consultants* is published twice a year as an updating
service.

186. *Consumer Sourcebook*. Detroit, Michigan: Gale Research Company. NOTE: Find out where to go, who to
telephone or see for virtually any kind of consumer
concern. The *Sourcebook* is

> a directory and guide to government organizations; as-
> sociations, centers and institutes; media services;
> company and trademark information; and bibliographic
> material relating to consumer topics, sources of re-
> course, and advisory information.

Other consumer directories include the *Reference
Guide For Consumers,* published by the R.R. Bowker
Company, and the *Consumer Protection Directory,*
published by Marquis Academic Media.

187. *A Directory of Information Resources in the United
States*. Washington, D.C.: Government Printing Office. NOTE: The Library of Congress, National Refer-
ral Center, regularly revises and reissues several
parts to this directory. They include volumes for the
biological sciences, federal government, physical
sciences and engineering, and social sciences. With
these you can identify government-sponsored information sources, as well as the information sources of

the federal government itself. Most of these sources will answer your questions via the mail, by telephone, or in person.

188. *Directory of Special Libraries and Information Centers*. Detroit, Michigan: Gale Research Company. NOTE: The basic volume includes library names, addresses, telephone numbers, names of key personnel, and other information. A periodic supplement covering the time between editions of the basic volume keep the directory up-to-date. There is also a "Geographic-Personnel Index" volume. the Gale Research Company publishes this same directory in a five-volume subject breakdown. It contains every entry from the basic volume, reorganized according to subject. Check *Subject Collections* (item 199) for specific information on special collections of material within libraries. The *American Library Directory* (item 183) is a general library guide.

189. *The Directory of World Museums*. New York: Columbia University Press, 1975. NOTE: Researcher-writers, scholars, collectors, artists, travelers, and museum buffs will find this guide useful. Its coverage is more comprehensive than the second edition of the *Museums Directory of the United States and Canada* published in 1965 by the American Association of Museums and the Smithsonian Institute. You will still find the older directory in most libraries. Its descriptions of museums, although dated, are more inclusive than those in *The Directory of World Museums*.

190. *Encyclopedia of Associations*. Detroit, Michigan: Gale Research Company . NOTE: The latest edition of this frequently revised directory lists thousands of organized groups in the United States. Listings include names and addresses, descriptions of purposes and

activities, references to publications, dates for conventions or meetings, and other data. Many of the services and publications described are available at nominal cost or entirely free. The basic volume is kept up-to-date by "New Associations and Projects," a supplement issued quarterly. There is also a separate "Geographic and Executive Index" volume.

191. *Encyclopedia of Governmental Advisory Organizations*. Detroit, Michigan: Gale Research Company. NOTE: This is

> a reference guide to Presidential advisory committees, public advisory committees, interagency committees, and other government-related boards, panels, task forces, commissions, conferences, and other similar bodies serving in a consultative, coordinating, advisory, research, or investigative capacity.

New Governmental Advisory Organizations is a periodic supplement that keeps the *Encyclopedia* up-to-date.

192. *Environment U.S.A.* New York: R.R. Bowker Company. NOTE: Agencies, organizations, and individuals involved in environmental affairs are listed. Entries include names, addresses, telephone numbers, names of key personnel, and more. The *World Directory of Environmental Education Programs* and the *World Directory of Environmental Research Centers* are also distributed by the R.R. Bowker Company. The *Environmental Protection Directory* is published by Marquis Academic Media.

193. *The Foundation Directory*. New York: Columbia University Press. NOTE: Here is the major source of reference information in the field. It is prepared by the Foundation Center and describes major foundations in detail, including financial summaries.

Semiannual supplements list updated information available from the Foundation Center. There is also *The International Foundation Directory,* published in London by Europa Publications and distributed in the United States by the Gale Research Company.

194. *Guide to American Directories.* Detroit, Michigan: Gale Research Company. NOTE: Frequently revised, this is the most comprehensive key to the existence of directories covering business, industrial, professional, and commercial fields. It will lead you to an unbelievable range of indispensable information.

195. *Industrial Research Laboratories of the United States.*

New York: R.R. Bowker Company. NOTE: For over fifty years the various editions of this directory have been the single most valuable guide to the people and projects of U.S. research endeavors. Names of organizations, addresses, telephone numbers, names of key personnel, and descriptive profiles of each laboratory are all included. Indexes by geographical location, personnel, and subject give you quick access to the companies you want to know about. Check the *Research Centers Directory* (item 197) for a guide to university related and other nonprofit research centers.

196. *Picture Sources.* New York: Special Libraries Association. NOTE: Each new edition of this directory lists special collections of prints and photographs located in the United States and Canada. Most of the collections are generally available for reference use or publication. Another convenient picture source directory is included in the *Writer's Market* (item 225). Illustrations included in books and magazines are indexed alphabetically in the *Illustration Index,* published by Scarecrow Press.

197. *Research Centers Directory.* Detroit, Michigan: Gale

Research Company. NOTE: Virtually all university related and other nonprofit research centers in the United States and Canada are listed. Entries include names, addresses, and telephone numbers of research units, names of key personnel, and descriptive profiles of the organizations. *New Research Centers,* a supplement to the *Directory,* is published periodically by the Gale Research Company. Check *Industrial Research Laboratories of the United States* (item 195) as a guide to the research and development industry.

198. *SportSource.* Mountain View, California: World Publications, 1975. NOTE: This ambitious guide will help you discover the fascinating world of over two hundred sports. Its coverage ranges through the alphabet from abalone diving to yoga. It includes physical sport such as handball and mental sport such as checkers. The descriptions of each sport include a basic introduction and an essay written by a prominent participant in the sport. A directory at the end of each section, "For More Information," has the names and addresses of important information and equipment sources. Hundreds of photographic and graphic drawing illustrations make this a conversation piece as well as an information directory.

199. *Subject Collections.* New York: R.R. Bowker Company. NOTE: Each new and expanded edition provides all the information needed to locate, assess, and use special book and manuscript collections available in the United States and Canada. Check the *Directory of Special Libraries and Information Centers* (item 188) for a list of special libraries. The *American Library Directory* (item 183) is a general library guide.

200. *Thomas Register of American Manufacturers.* New

York: Thomas Publishing Company, annual. NOTE: Find the manufacturer of just about every product available through this multivolume directory. The information is conveniently arranged alphabetically by product. Business and commercial directories published by other companies include several manuals published by Moody's Investors Service, Inc., which give the facts and figures you need to make investment, financial, and marketing decisions. Dun & Bradstreet publishes standard marketing reference directories. Ask your librarian for further assistance when you must identify other business information sources.

201. *Washington Information Directory*. Washington, D.C.: Congressional Quarterly, Inc. NOTE: Here is

a road map through the bureaucracy of Washington, D.C. It places the names, telephone numbers, addresses and responsibilities of more than 5,000 key personnel and agencies—both governmental and private—at your fingertips, all indexed by subject.

For additional directory assistance in locating the sources of U.S. Gonvernment information, use the following as appropriate: *Congressional Staff Directory* (item 145); *Official Congressional Directory* (item 146); the *Federal Directory* (formerly called the *Federal Telephone Directory); the United States Government Manual* (item 124); and *A Directory of Information Resources in the United States* (item 187).

202. *Women's Movement Media: A Source Guide*. New York: R.R. Bowker Company, 1975. NOTE: Here is the most comprehensive, descriptive directory of the organizations, publications, products, and activities of the women's movement in the United

States and Canada. Find names, addresses, telephone numbers, key personnel, and much more. If you want to know who is doing what in the women's movement, check the latest edition of the *Women's Organization & Leaders Directory,* published by Today Publications & News Service Inc., National Press Building, Washington, D.C. 20004.

13. Markets for Your Work

Where will you publish your work? This is a natural question following an arduous research project and valuable time spent in writing an accurate piece you believe is a real contribution. But there is no easy answer. Librarians will seldom be able to help you much in your search for new and acceptable markets. Of course there are entire books written on how you should go about it. The trick is in finding a magazine or book publisher that will publish *your* work.

In addition to the "how-to" manuals on marketing your article or book, there are many market guides and directories. Some are written specifically for writers, such as the popular *Writer's Market* (item 225) or *Literary Market Place* (item 218). Others are compiled for booksellers, librarians, and scholars. If used in a different way than that for which they were intended, these other directories may be more satisfactory for your particular needs. For example, catalogs such as *Books In Print* (item 54), *Forthcoming Books In Print* (item 66), or *Publishers' Trade List Annual* (item 68) present useful surveys of what books are being published by which publishers. Or *Ulrich's International Periodicals Directory* (item 223) will identify more magazines on more subjects than all the writer's market directories combined.

Spend some time with the guides and directories list in this chapter. From them you will identify all the people, publishers, and services that may help you get into print.

203. *American Book Trade Directory*. New York: R.R. Bowker Company, biennial. NOTE: Locate names, addresses, and telephone numbers for thousands of active booksellers, publishers, and wholesalers. The lists include those located in the United States, Canada, Great Britain, and Ireland. Two other valuable features are lists of bookstores and their specialties and a list of greeting card publishers.

204. *Artist's Market*. Cincinnati, Ohio: Writer's Digest. NOTE: From the publishers of the annual *Writer's Market* (item 225). This reference book lists over two-thousand current outlets where artists, photographers, illustrators, and cartoonists can sell their work.

205. *Audiovisual Market Place: A Multimedia Guide*. New York: R.R. Bowker Company, biennial. NOTE:

Designed for those in the market for AV materials, this convenient guide provides company names, addresses, key personnel and product lines for all active producers, distributors, and other sources of AV learning materials.

An annotated bibliography of AV reference works and a directory of AV magazines are also included.

206. *Ayer Directory of Publications*. Philadelphia, Pennsylvania: Ayer Press, annual. NOTE: The *Ayer Directory* is a geographic listing intended as

a basic, authoritative reference tool to which professionals will be inclined to turn first for the current, accurate, and useful information relating to newspapers, magazines, trade and professional publications.

It is not comprehensive. For publications not included, check *The Standard Periodical Directory* (item 222) or *Ulrich's International Periodicals Directory* (item 223).

207. Camp, William L., and Schwark, Bryan L. *Guide to Periodicals in Education and Its Academic Disciplines*. Metuchen, New Jersey: Scarecrow Press, Inc. NOTE: Since 1968, when the first edition of this guide was published, research-writers in the education field have found it immensely useful. Its primary purpose is to provide editorial and manuscript information for writers who wish to submit articles for publication. A similar guide published by The Scarecrow Press is *Education/Psychology Journals: A Scholars Guide*. It also gives the editorial requirements for those journals to which you may want to send a manuscript. See also: *Writer's Market* (item 225), *Directory of Publishing Opportunities* (item 210), and *Scholars Market* (item 215).

208. *Contemporary Crafts Market Place*. New York: R.R. Bowker Company, biennial. NOTE: Compiled by the American Crafts Council, this is the most comprehensive guide in the field. With it you can locate information about people, organizations, suppliers, and services. There is also a list of reference books for every craft, and a special directory of craft magazines.

209. *Directory of the College Student Press in America*. New York: Oxbridge Publishing Co., Inc., biennial. NOTE: Campus publications from every state are listed. Each listing includes financial data, circulation statistics, typographical information, and editorial descriptions.

210. *Directory of Publishing Opportunities*. Chicago: Marquis Academic Media. NOTE: There is no better guide

to publishing opportunities in the major academic, research, scholarly, and technical fields. Specific manuscript information is given for hundreds of publications that accept articles. Every aspect of article preparation and submission is included, from journal title, editor and address, to payment arrangements. New editions are published periodically. See also: *Guide to Periodicals in Education and Its Academic Disciplines* (item 207), *Scholars Market* (item 215), and *Writer's Market* (item 225).

211. *The Dobler World Directory of Youth Periodicals*. New York: Citation Press. NOTE: Writers, illustrators, editors, publishers, librarians, and teachers have found the several editions of this guide to be the only comprehensive listing of periodicals published specifically for children and teenagers. Editors, addresses, and editorial information are given for each listing.

212. *Editor & Publisher International Year Book*. New York: Editor & Publisher, annual. NOTE: This "encyclopedia of the newspaper industry" lists all American and foreign daily and weekly newspapers. Each listing presents the names of executives and editors as well as publication and circulation data. There are also lists of news services, syndicates, advertising agencies, and related newspaper publishing enterprises. For a complete list of syndicates check the *Editor & Publisher Syndicate Directory*. For facts and figures on the characteristics of population, retail sales, education, climate, and income in a newspaper's geographical area, check the *Editor & Publisher Market Guide*. The weekly *Editor & Publisher* magazine will keep you informed of all the latest developments in the newspaper industry.

213. *Fine Arts Market Place*. New York: R.R. Bowker

Company, biennial. NOTE: Locate services, organizations and associations, dealers, publishers, suppliers, and more, all in this single source. It includes the names, addresses, telephone numbers and areas of special interest for thousands of individuals and firms.

214. *Gebbie House Magazine Directory*. Burlington, Iowa: National Research Bureau, Inc. NOTE: According to this directory

> a house magazine is a publication that carries no paid advertising, is given free to its readers, and is produced by a company, firm, association or even an individual with the completely frank intention of promoting the sponsor's interest.

Next to *Writer's Market* (item 225) this is the single most valuable directory for free-lance writers. New editions are published periodically to give exact data on which house magazines use what kind of material. If you are unfamiliar with the market, a survey of this guide will open new ideas for your work. A valuable "Questions and Answers" section on the field is included at the back of the volume.

215. Harmon, Gary L., and Harmon, Susanna M. *Scholar's Market: An International Directory of Periodicals Publishing Literary Scholarship*. Columbus, Ohio: Publications Committee, The Ohio State University Libraries, A Division of Educational Services, 1974. NOTE: *Scholar's Market* is the first comprehensive guide to publishing opportunities in periodicals of all types that publish literary criticism, history, or bibliography. Each of the 848 listings includes an editorial address, a description of contents, and an explanation of editorial and manuscript requirements. If you cannot find the right market for your work in

this guide, check the *Directory of Publishing Opportunities* (item 210).

216. *International Academic and Specialist Publisher's Directory*. New York: R.R. Bowker Company. NOTE: First issued in 1975, this directory will help you identify, locate, and learn the subject specialties of some ten-thousand publishers throughout the world. The subjects covered include a broad range from esoteric to popular.

217. *International Directory of Little Magazines and Small Presses*. Paradise, California: Dustbooks, annual. NOTE: Writers, editors, and publishers are brought together with the aid of this essential directory. Listings include the names of editors with addresses, descriptions of material published, frequency of publication, method of production, payment rates, and other data. Another guide to small publishers is *Alternatives In Print: An Index and Listing of Some Movement Publications Reflecting Todays' Social Change Activities*. It is published by the Office of Educational Services, The Ohio State University Libraries.

218. *Literary Market Place*. New York: R.R. Bowker Company, annual. NOTE: This is the standard directory for the world of American book publishing. It includes names and addresses of book publishers, manufacturers, agents and agencies, review media, and related services. In addition to this essential guide, check *Writer's Market* (item 225).

219. *The Mediamatic Calendar of Special Editorial Issues*. New York: Media/Distribution Services, Inc., three times per year. NOTE: Use this unique calendar to specifically plan your writing projects months in advance. It tells what topics will be featured in trade, technical and professional journals, as well as con-

sumer magazines. Editorial and advertising closing dates are noted. Although designed for public relations practitioners in agencies and corporations, *The Mediamatic Calendar* and other Mediamatic System services will provide imaginative writers with an unusual marketing key. Write for free information about the Mediamatic System to: Media / Distribution Services, Inc., 423 West 55th Street, New York, NY 10019.

220. O'Neill, Carol L ., and Ruder, Avima. *The Complete Guide to Editorial Freelancing*. New York: Dodd, Mead & Company, 1974. NOTE: Most of the book tells how to be successful at freelancing, copyediting, proofreading, indexing, and other editorial work. A guide to "The Freelance Job Market," Appendix IV, tells you where to market your skills.

221. *Photography Market Place*. New York: R.R. Bowker Company, biennial. NOTE: Here is the best directory of picture buyers, custom laboratories, model agencies, supply houses, grants and awards, and other services that every photographer needs. It provides names, addresses, telephone numbers, and thousands of other facts essential for photographic buying and selling.

222. *The Standard Periodical Directory*. New York: Oxbridge Publishing Co., Inc. NOTE: Find out what periodicals are being published. It covers magazines, journals, newspapers, newsletters, house magazines, and government publications. All are arranged by subject. There is an alphabetical index of titles. *Ulrich's International Periodicals Directory* (item 223) is more commonly available in libraries.

223. *Ulrich's International Periodicals Directory*. New York: R.R. Bowker Company, biennial. NOTE: Commonly called "*Ulrich's*," this is the outstanding

directory of its kind. Arranged by subject, it is an essential research guide as well as a directory to potential magazine article markets. There is an index of titles. Check *The Standard Periodical Directory* (item 222) if you cannot find what you want in *Ulrich's*. The R.R. Bowker Company also publishes *Irregular Serials and Annuals,* a valuable aid in researching publications issued irregularly or less frequently than twice a year.

224. *Working Press of the Nation*. Burlington, Iowa: National Research Bureau, annual. NOTE: Here is the most comprehensive roster of press, news service, feature syndicates, and other important management and editorial personnel available anywhere. It includes names, titles, addresses, and telephone numbers of key individuals you may wish to reach. Four volumes cover newspapers, magazines, radio and television, and feature writers and syndicates.

225. *Writer's Market*. Cincinnati, Ohio: Writer's Digest, annual. NOTE: American free-lance writers rely on this directory more than any other in order to find paying markets for articles, short stories, novels, nonfiction books, plays, poetry, gags, and photographs. There are over five-thousand different entries listed under over two-hundred categories. One section gives the names and addresses of literary agencies, and a special section is devoted entirely to newspaper syndicates. If you cannot find what you want in this standard handbook, check *Guide to Periodicals in Education and Its Academic Disciplines* (item 207), *Gebbie House Magazine Directory* (item 214), *Scholar's Market* (item 215), or *Directory of Publishing Opportunities* (item 210). Stay up-to-date on the latest market changes with the monthly issues of *Writer's Digest* or *The Writer*. The *Writer's*

Digest supplements *Writer's Market*. *The Writer* includes a regular "Market News" section, a "Market Newsletter," and other special lists to help writers find suitable markets for their manuscripts. The British publishing market is described in the annual *Writer's & Artists' Yearbook*.

14. Contests, Awards, Financial Aid

Looking for further recognition of your work? Need money for research? Want to enter writing contests that pay? Numerous literary prizes, writing awards, and research grants are available and waiting for your application.

You may have to look in a variety of sources to find the right contest or grant for your particular manuscript or research. For example, "Contests and Awards" are listed in *Writer's Market* (item 225), with supplementary lists included in *Writer's Digest* magazine. *The Writer* magazine also lists contests and awards.

Literary Market Place (item 218) lists contests as well as literary fellowships and grants. The *Editor & Publisher International Year Book* (item 212) lists contests and awards for newspaper journalism.

In addition to these sources and the reference books listed below, your librarian can show you other directories to scholarships, fellowships, and research grants.

226. *Annual Register of Grant Support*. Chicago: Marquis Academic Media. NOTE: Each annual revision identifies current grants, fellowships, travel and construction grants, scholarships, awards, and prizes. List-

ings include complete information on qualification criteria and application procedures.

227. *Awards, Honors, and Prizes.* Detroit, Michigan: Gale Research Company. NOTE: Each listing provides details on how an award is earned, how often it is presented, and what recognition or financial rewards are attached. There is an alphabetical index and a subject index of awards. Revised periodically.

228. *Directory of Research Grants.* Scottsdale, Arizona: The Oryx Press, annual. NOTE: All the data essential for securing funds for study and research is organized conveniently by academic discipline and deadline dates. It is indexed by grant name, sponsoring organization, and sponsoring organization by type.

229. *The Grants Register.* New York: St. Martin's Press, biennial. NOTE: Identify grants for study, creative work, projects, or training. Each listing includes a description of the award, number offered, value, eligibility requirements, closing dates, and other application information. The final section of the book summarizes other reference publications in the field.

15. Tips for the Researcher-Writer

230. Reference Librarians. NOTE: A good reference librarian knows what material is in a library and where it is found, or at least how to find it. Don't assume that any library employee can help you. Nor can you depend on just any librarian. Make the acquaintance of an expert reference librarian in whom you have confidence. A competent reference librarian's intimate knowledge of reference resources will make your research easier and more productive. And on a deadline your librarian may be the best friend you have.

231. Organize Your Library Research. NOTE: *First,* do not make a trip to the library every time you require information. Rely on your personal reference library (item 243) as a matter of convenience. Or telephone a library for facts such as dates, addresses, specific statistics, or confirmation that the library has certain material. Cumulate other library research needs and plan one trip to the library to do the work. *Second,* copy all the data on references (source, page number, etc.) as you find them. This will eliminate the need for retracing the same research to find what you

missed the first time. You will also have the reference at hand for later footnoting. Or to show where your information came from should it later be questioned by an editor or publisher. Or as a reference should your material be challenged for authenticity and/or accuracy by an alert reader. *Third,* keep a record of the reference materials you check in order to avoid repeating searches in the same sources. It's easy to become lost in a maze of data in the middle of a literature research project, so be extremely methodical in your record keeping.

232. Library Card Catalogs. NOTE: Dispel the notion that knowledge of how to use the card catalog is the only knowhow you must have when doing library research. Card catalogs are incapable of showing, explaining, and relating to one another the many information sources available. They are also notorious for not being up-to-date and for excluding material other than books. Card catalogs are most useful for locating books by specific authors or titles. You can also look up books by subject, although a catalog will frequently fail to "think of subjects" as you would. So, *ask your librarian* for assistance when you cannot find what you want in the card catalog!

233. Indexes to Magazines. NOTE: Don't limit your magazine index research to that familiar old standby, the *Readers' Guide to Periodical Literature* (item 18). There are indexes and abstracting services for numerous specific subjects. Check Chapter 2 in this book to learn what they are.

234. Compiling a Bibliography. NOTE: After deciding on a topic about which you intend to write, you must usually set about collecting a list of books and articles on the subject. Don't limit yourself to the card catalog (item 232) when collecting the bibliography.

Check such references as *Bibliographic Index* (item 53) or the appropriate indexes and abstracts listed in Chapter 2 of this book. Also locate bibliographies included in encyclopedias and other reference books. And don't forget to consult with your librarian in order to ensure that nothing is overlooked. After you have compiled a bibliography, utilize the interlibrary loan system (item 236) to retrieve material not in your library.

235. Computer-Based Bibliographic Research. NOTE: If money is no object, you will save considerable time by purchasing an automated literature search. Most large academic research libraries and some special libraries now offer such a service. The research is usually based on familiar references such as *Chemical Abstracts* (item 33) or *Psychological Abstracts* (item 36). The computer will work for you by quickly sorting, selecting, and delivering a bibliography of citations. Ask your librarian for additional information about these time-saving programs.

236. Interlibrary Loan. NOTE: As with the "yellow pages," an interlibrary loan service will "do the walking" for you if you need material from another library. Subject to the Interlibrary Loan Code of the American Library Association, you can make a request at your local library and within a week or two have the material in hand.

237. Compile a Local Information Source File. NOTE: Develop a file of special information sources in your local area. Include such sources as public, academic, and special libraries; private libraries and commercial or business information centers; historical societies, clubs, and civic organizations; museums and art galleries; the chamber of commerce and tourist bureau; and churches and religious groups.

The telephone directory yellow pages will give you some leads. Or check the directories listed in Chapter 12 of this book. Also, read you local newspaper for leads to individuals or agencies who are recognized as authorities in a given field.

238. Copyright. NOTE: Write for free information about copyright laws and application procedures: Copyright Office, Library of Congress, Washington, D.C. 20559. The Copyright Office will send you copyright applications for everything from a book or a painting to a photograph or a musical composition. Free booklets are also available, such as, "How to Investigate the Copyright Status of a Work," "Regulations of the Copyright Office," and "General Information on Copyright." Ask for a list of all available materials. Then request the specific items you want. Every researcher-writer should have a special file devoted to copyright.

239. Doctoral Dissertations. NOTE: These are comprehensive treatments of specialized topics. The bibliographies included are particularly useful as material for other work. Dissertations are seldom listed in the usual book trade catalogs. So, ask your librarian for assistance in locating and using a series of special catalogs that do list them. These include *Dissertation Abstracts International* and *Dissertation Abstracts International Retrospective Index,* which are published by Xerox University Microfilms. In many cases you can request and receive dissertations through your interlibrary loan service (item 236). Or, copies are available for sale by Xerox University Microfilms, Ann Arbor, Michigan 48106. Write them for free lists and catalogs of dissertations, theses, books, and serials available from the company.

240. Other Unique Writer's Research Guides.

Downs, Robert B. & Keller, Clara D. *How to Do Library Research*. Urbana, Illinois: University of Illinois Press, 2nd ed., 1975.

Gates, Jean Key. *Guide to the Use of Books and Libraries*. New York: McGraw-Hill Book Company, 3rd ed., 1973.

McCoy, F.N. *Researching and Writing in History: A Practical Handbook for Students*. Berkeley, California: University of California Press, 1974.

Rivers, William L. *Finding Facts; Interviewing, Observing, Using Reference Sources*. Englewood Cliffs, New Jersey: Prentice-Hall, Inc. 1975.

Todd, Alden. *Finding Facts Fast: How to Find Out What You Want to Know Immediately*. New York: William Morrow & Company, Inc., 1972.

241. Lead Files. NOTE: Subcribe to a variety of newspapers and magazines. Or, purchase them regularly from newsstands. Scan these publications and clip out the articles that are worth filing for future reference. For example, *Playboy* and *Penthouse* regularly publish in-depth interviews with major political figures, well-known authors, or other highly recognizable celebrities. Such interview material is an invaluable information source for future reference—and it will be readily available if you have it in your own lead files. *Reader's Digest* is one of the best magazines available for topical information. The *Christian Science Monitor, The National Observer,* and the *National Enquirer* are unique newspapers but frequently overlooked. Each is packed with good material well worth clipping and filing. And remember, all the money you invest in newspaper and magazine subscriptions, or single purchases, is tax deductible.

242. Build a Personal Reference Library. NOTE: This will take time but it can be done easily without great

expense. Consider the paperback editions listed in
Reference Books in Paperback (item 44) or
Paperbound Books in Print (item 57). Or, simply join
one or more of the book clubs listed in *Literary
Market Place* (item 218) or the *American Book
Trade Directory* (item 203). Better yet, get on the
mailing lists of some of the major discount book-sales
firms that sell by mail at substantial savings. You'll
find some listed under "Remainder Dealers" in
Literary Market Place (item 218) or the *American
Book Trade Directory* (item 203). Or try this one:
Publisher's Central Bureau, 1 Champion Avenue,
Avenel, New Jersey 07131. They will regularly send
you sale catalogs with price reductions of up to
ninety percent on new books. It is one of the best
sources for very expensive reference books — inex-
pensively priced. For example, you can sometimes
pick up such bargins as the *Celebrity Register* for
one-third its regular retail price. Hobby and crafts
books are frequently listed, as well as good books on
the arts, history, religion, and other subjects.
Remember! All your book purchases are tax deductible as a business expense for writers or would-
be writers.

243. Taxes for Writers. **NOTE:** The special income tax breaks
given to writers are vast and complicated. Every
researcher-writer should find a good accountant who
has knowledge of the tax laws involved. The fly-by-
night income tax consultants who open a store-front
office or set up shop in a trailer for a few months each
year will not do! Nor will the mass marketing tax
return businesses such as H&R Block. They have
neither the time nor the inclination to prepare the
necessary in-depth tax return you should have. In-
quire of various tax accountants to learn if they have

the experience necessary for preparing the kind of income tax return you need. Should you not find a competent tax accountant locally, write to: Clyde E. English, Public Accountant, 4130 Atlantic Avenue, Long Beach, California 90807. This particular accountant specializes in tax returns for show-business personalities and writers. For additional information you should have on file two special articles, which appeared in *Reader's Digest*. Read: "What to Do If You Disagree With the IRS," March, 1972, pages 133-136; and "If Your Tax Return Is Audited," April, 1973, pages 151-154. Copies of these articles may be made for your use with self-service photocopy machines in most libraries.

244. Writer's Guidlines. NOTE: In addition to developing lead files (item 241), write to various publishers and request "writer's guidelines" and sample copies of magazines. For example, National Features Syndicate will send you a booklet entitled "Guidelines for Freelancers; How You Can Sell To Us At Top Dollar!" Or you can obtain a free copy of "Guidelines and Rates of Payment for Free-Lance Contributors to *Horseman, The Magazine of Western Riding*." Globe Communication Corporation (*Midnight* newspaper) will send "A Guide to Freelancers" and "Preparing Your Manuscript." *Farm Wife News* will send you excellent material entitled "Guide For Freelancers." But the best guide available is probably that from *Seventy Six* magazine. They will generously send on request what amounts to a complete course in freelance writing. You'll find addresses for these publishers and hundreds more in *Writer's Market* (item 225), the *Gebbie House Magazine Directory* (item 214), and *Ulrich's International Periodicals Directory* (item 223).

245. Library Handbooks. NOTE: Ask your librarian for a copy of the library's handbook. These guides to collections and services are published by most larger libraries. For example, The University of Tennessee, Knoxville, publishes "Your Libraries," and The University of South Carolina issues a "Library Handbook." They are designed to help you use the library and are free for the asking.

246. The Metric System. NOTE: "America *is* going metric!" Major industries and organizations are already converting, and researcher-writers must keep up with the conversion. The most complete and up-to-date documentation on the subject is available from the technical publication firm, J.J. Keller & Associates, Inc. Their "Metric System Guide Library" updates and contains all the information necessary to fully understand the background of metric conversion in America. Write and request further information from: J.J. Keller & Associates, Inc., 145 West Wisconsin Avenue, Neenay, Wisconsin 54956.